CHICKEN SOUP FOR THE SOUL
A TRIBUTE TO MOMS

CHICKEN SOUP FOR THE SOUL A TRIBUTE TO MOMS

Jack Canfield
Mark Victor Hansen
Patty Aubery

Health Communications, Inc.
Deerfield Beach, Florida

www.hcibooks.com
www.chickensoup.com

We would like to acknowledge the many publishers and individuals who granted us permission to reprint the cited material.

Cappuccino Tacos and Bubble Pie. Reprinted by permission of Celeste Titcomb Palermo. ©2007 Celeste Titcomb Palermo.

Best Friends. Reprinted by permission of Jennifer Lynn Clay. ©2005 Jennifer Lynn Clay.

Tea for Two. Reprinted by permisson of Terri Elders. ©2007 Terri Elders.

Faster than Speeding Bullet. Reprinted by permission of Sarah Rutherford Smiley. ©2006 Sarah Rutherford Smiley.

(Continued on page 244)

Library of Congress Cataloging-in-Publication Data
is available through the Library of Congress.

© 2008 John T. Canfield and Hansen and Hansen LLC
ISBN-13: 978-7573-0664-8
ISBN-10: 0-7573-0664-0

Publisher: Health Communications, Inc.
         3201 S.W. 15th Street
         Deerfield Beach, FL 33442-8190

Cover design by Andrea Perrine Brower
Inside formatting by Dawn Von Strolley Grove

This book is simply and lovingly
dedicated to all the moms in world.

Thanks, Mom

Contents

Acknowledgments

We wish to express our heartfelt gratitude to all of the people who helped make this book possible:

Our families, who have been chicken soup for our souls by supporting us as we continue to serve our readers endlessly.

Our publisher and friend, Peter Vegso, for his continuous support and allegiance to all of us and to the Chicken Soup brand.

Russ Kamalski, for being there during every step of the journey, with love, laughter, and endless creativity.

D'ette Corona and Barbara LoMonaco, who both seamlessly manage twenty to thirty projects at a time.

Patty Hansen, for her thorough and competent handling of the legal and licensing aspects of Chicken Soup for the Soul books. You are magnificent at the challenge!

Veronica Romero, Lisa Williams, Teresa Collett, Robin Yerian, Jesse Ianniello, Lauren Edelstein, Lauren Bray, Patti Clement, Laurie Hartman, Connie Simoni, Karen Schoenfeld, Marty Robinson, Debbie Lefever, Patti Coffey, Pat Burns, Kristi Waite, and Blake Arce, who support Jack's and Mark's businesses with skill and love.

Michele Matrisciani, Carol Rosenberg, Andrea Gold, Allison Janse, and Katheline St. Fort, our editors at Health

Communications, Inc., for their devotion to excellence.

Brian Peluso and the rest of the warehouse shipping staff who make certain that deliveries are made.

Pat Holdsworth, Doreen Hess, Terry York, Lori Golden, Veronica Blake, Kelly Maragni, Sean Geary, Gina Johnson, Mike Briggs, Patricia McConnell, Lisa Baxter, Kim Weiss, Paola Fernandez-Rana, Christine Zambrano, and Jaron Hunter for doing such an incredible job supporting our books.

Tom Sand, Lorrie Keip, Claude Choquette, Marielle Lemay, and Luc Jutras, who manage year after year to get our books translated into thirty-six languages around the world.

Larissa Hise Henoch, Andrea Perrine Brower, Anthony Clausi, Lawna Patterson Oldfield, Justin Rotkowitz, Peter Quintal, and Dawn Von Strolley Grove for their talent, creativity, and unrelenting patience while producing book covers and inside designs that capture the essence of Chicken Soup.

Ken and Dahlynn McKowen, for editing the final manuscript with such enthusiasm. Your willingness to help and your friendship means the world to all of us.

To everyone who submitted a story, we deeply appreciate your letting us into your lives and sharing your experiences with us. For those whose stories were not chosen for publication, we hope the stories you are about to enjoy convey what was in your heart and in some ways also tell your story.

Because of the size of this project, we may have left out the names of some people who contributed along the way. If so, we are sorry, but please know that we really do appreciate you very much.

We are truly grateful and love you all!

Introduction

M-O-T-H-E-R

"M" is for the million things she gave me,
"O" means only that she's growing old,
"T" is for the tears she shed to save me,
"H" is for her heart of purest gold;
"E" is for her eyes, with love-light shining,
"R" means right, and right she'll always be,
    Put them all together, they spell "MOTHER,"
    A word that means the world to me.

Howard Johnson

How many times have you wanted to tell your mother how you really felt about her, like Howard Johnson does in his ode above? Granted, not all of us are poet laureates, but it's not necessary to be one to show your mother how much you care for her. A simple hug or kiss would thrill your mother to no end, guaranteed.

That's what the contributors to this very special book have done. Through their inspiring, moving, and often funny stories, poems, and cartoons, they all pay tribute to their mothers, and their contributions to this very special tribute book speak volumes about their love and admiration for the special person each calls "Mom."

We invite you to share in their memories and to rekindle the memories in your own life. And if you're still finding it hard to come up with the right words to tell your mom how much you love her, there's a solution: hand her this book, give her that hug or kiss, and simply say, "Thanks, Mom."

Share with Us

We would love to hear your reactions to the stories in this book. Please let us know what your favorite stories were and how they affected you.

We also invite you to send us stories you would like to see published in future editions of Chicken Soup for the Soul. Please send submissions to:

www.chickensoup.com
Chicken Soup for the Soul
P.O. Box 30880
Santa Barbara, CA 93130
fax: 805-563-2945

You can also access e-mail or find a current list of planned books at the Chicken Soup for the Soul website at www.chickensoup.com. Find out about our Internet service at www.clubchickensoup.com.

We hope you enjoy reading this book as much as we enjoyed compiling, editing, and writing it.

1

SPECIAL MOMENTS

We do not know the true value of our moments until they have undergone the test of memory.

George Duhamel

Cappuccino Tacos and Bubble Pie

*Give love and unconditional acceptance to
those you encounter, and notice what happens.*

Wayne Dyer

When the lavender-scented bubbles reached the crest
of the tub, I turned off the faucet.

"I'm going to take a bath," I hollered to my husband.
"Can you watch Peyton for a few minutes?"

"Sure. I'll try," answered a distant voice.

I sank into the tub, took a deep breath, and started to let
the bombardments of life melt away. And then the bathroom door creaked open.

The blue eyes of my three-year-old daughter peeked
into my private haven.

"Mommy, can I come in?" Peyton whispered, her voice
tentative and polite. She stood like a soldier, awaiting
orders.

"Oh, okay, just for a minute," I grumbled, and she scur-
ried into the room, beaming.

"Is it hot?" she inquired, casually dipping her finger into
the water to gauge the temperature.

"Yes. It's hot, very hot," I said, hoping to discourage her

invasion of my bath. "Mommy likes it that way."

"Oh," she sighed, disappointed. She was crestfallen the water was not in her temperature range, but knew that there was a remedy. "Can I get in with you?"

I growled and furrowed my brow, teasing her. "Okay, okay," I said, adding cold water from the tap. She shimmied out of her pajamas and practically dove in.

"I'm going to make you cappuccino tacos and bubble pie," Peyton announced as she spread a handful of bubbles onto a washcloth.

"Sounds delicious. Those are my favorites," I answered with only my head above the tepid water.

"Do you want milk or juice?" she asked.

"Will you make me a milkshake?"

"Oh, yes," my little chef replied. "Do you want vanilla or chocolate?"

"Chocolate."

"Do you want whipped cream and sprinkles?"

"Of course. That's the only way to have a milkshake, right?"

"Yep," she agreed as she added a dollop of whipped-cream bubbles and pretend sprinkles, sprinkles of love.

Peyton's encroachment on my bathtime has become a ritual in our home over the years. And to be honest, at first I really missed my solo dip—when I could read a magazine and let the stress of the day dissolve into the scalding water sans distraction. But life has taught me not to fritter away these precious moments of motherhood.

When she was five, Peyton was diagnosed with a brain tumor. She spent a month in the hospital and I routinely would climb into her metal-frame bed, sharing cafeteria-issue milkshakes with her—longing for a lukewarm bath, a frothy bubble pie, and the sweet taste of more time.

These days, Peyton's foamy milkshakes top my list of favorites. When she serves up her creative bubble-concoctions, she always reminds me to give thanks. So we bow our heads together and pray.

I am thankful for so much more than these frothy bath-time concoctions.

Celeste T. Palermo

Best Friends

Golden sunlight streams through the little window.
Our heads are bowed so close together
that the same ray of sunshine highlights our hair.
We whisper, then giggle.
The two of us act so much like young schoolgirls
that no one would ever guess
we are mother and daughter
simply painting each other's toenails.

Jennifer Lynn Clay

Tea for Two

Every problem has a gift for you in its hands.

Richard Bach

My sequined purple princess costume remained in its tissue paper wrappings on the top shelf of my bedroom closet, as I perched in my pink flannel pajamas on the window seat, peering out the bay window at the neighborhood witches, ghosts, and cowboys scurrying by.

On October 31, 1944, we didn't expect any knocks at our front door, festooned not with the jack-o'-lantern cutout I had made in my first-grade classroom the week before, but with a stark black-and-white quarantine sign that shouted, "Contagious Disease, Chicken Pox!"

Daddy had taken my unaffected older sister and little brother to Grandma's house for a party earlier that evening, leaving Mama and me home alone. I had finished reading all the stories in the newest edition of *Children's Activities,* tired of cutting out paper dolls from the old Sears catalog, and longed to be outside. Mama had promised me a special treat, but I couldn't imagine what could replace the thrill of joining the troops of children wandering door-to-door in the autumn twilight with their rapidly filling pillow slips. No Hershey bars, candied apples, or popcorn balls for me this year, I knew. *I don't care*, I told myself, because though the itching had ceased, I had yet to regain my appetite anyway.

I heard Mama turn on the radio in the kitchen, and then heard her call to me, "Time to get dressed!"

Glancing down at my pajamas, I wondered what she could mean, but scooted off my seat and trudged to the kitchen. On the back of one of the chrome dinette chairs hung Mama's fur chubby, a kind of short jacket that represented the essence of elegance to me those days. I used to love to watch Mama get dressed for special evenings, in her chiffon dresses always topped by the chubby.

"Put it on," she said, pointing to the jacket. "We are going to play tea party, and I am going to be the hostess, while you will be my guest." She draped a string of pearls around my neck, as I shrugged into the jacket. I noticed that the table had been set with her best Blue Willow cups and saucers, and that an empty platter had been placed next to the toaster.

Though I could not venture all the way out, Mama opened the door a crack so I could at least knock on the outside, right below the Quarantine sign. "Oh, Miss Terri, it's so good of you to call this evening. It's tea time," she announced. "And even though you are my guest, I'm going to ask you to make the meal, since you have such a special touch with cinnamon toast."

I'd seen the bakery truck make its delivery earlier, and had wondered what had been left on our doorstep. Now Mama opened the bread box and pulled out a loaf of sliced raisin bread. She placed the sugar bowl, the butter dish, and the red tin of cinnamon on the counter, and lifted the chubby from my shoulders. Then she opened her *Searchlight Recipe Book* to page forty-four, handed me the yellow plastic measuring spoon set, and said, "Let's see how you do reading that recipe."

I was the best reader in my class, so I stumbled only on "substitute" and "proportion" as I read aloud the instructions.

"Cinnamon Toast: Spread freshly toasted bread with butter or butter substitute. Spread generously with sugar and cinnamon which have been blended in the proportion of one teaspoon cinnamon to a half of cup sugar."

While I watched the raisin bread brown in our two-sided toaster, Mama put her tea kettle on to boil, and told me a story about the birds on the Blue Willow china. She said that an angry Chinese father had been trying to catch his daughter who was running away with a boyfriend. Before he could catch them, they had been transformed into birds and flew away together. I rubbed my finger across the birds on the saucer. "When you grow up, your father won't chase away your boyfriends," she said with a little laugh. "And now that you're learning to cook, it won't be too much longer before you are grown up for every day, not just for Halloween." I smiled. It was true. I was learning to cook.

Though I hadn't been hungry all day long, the smell of the cinnamon sugar seemed to reawaken my appetite, and I ate my entire slice and half of Mama's, and even managed a swallow or two of my milk tea. When my sister returned later that evening with the candied apples that Grandma had sent, I accepted one, but insisted I wasn't really hungry, since I had cooked and eaten a meal earlier.

Mama's prediction came true, too, as I became engaged just a dozen years later. And at my wedding shower in 1955, she presented me with a black leatherette bound *Searchlight Recipe Book*. I turn the yellowed pages today to page forty-four, and again recall the delicious aroma of cinnamon toast as I remember the year that trick or treat became tea for two.

Terri Elders

Faster than a Speeding Bullet

Trust yourself, you know more than you think you do.

Benjamin Spock

I was walking down our street the other day when I saw a little boy dressed in Superman pajamas toddling to the curb with his grandmother. The cape attached to his shoulders flapped in the wind like a cheap sheet. But he didn't care. With official Superman clothes hanging—and I do mean hanging—from his body, I knew the boy believed, without hesitation, that he could bend steel.

My two oldest boys, Ford, six, and Owen, four, spent a full year in Superman pajamas. I had to buy several sets just to keep up with the laundry. On Halloween, I begged them to pick different costumes. "Halloween is about pretending to be something you're not," I had said. "You're Superman every day; why not give Bert and Ernie a try?" It never worked. Ford was so convinced of his Superman-like traits, he styled his hair with one curl of bangs hanging in the front.

Today, Ford and Owen are what we call "closet"

Superman lovers. They'd rather be caught watching *Blue's Clues* than have a neighbor see them running down the driveway in their dress-up pajamas. But that doesn't mean they don't still covet Superman underwear. They're just a little more discreet. (Back in the day, Ford used to wear his red underwear on the outside of his pants, just to get a more genuine Superman effect. And I took him to the grocery store like that.)

A few years ago, when I washed Superman capes every single night, I thought the phase would never end. My ultimate fear was that Ford and Owen would one day wear blue tights and a red cape to high school. I began to worry that the alter-ego thing was messing with their heads. My husband and I set rules about how much time they could spend as Superman . . . until I gave that idea more thought. (Imagine a thirty-year-old sitting in his office, legs covered in shiny blue tights and propped on the desk, telling his secretary, "Jane, hold my calls; I've got ten more minutes as Superman.")

Just when I believed that we'd have to change Owen's name to Clark and Ford's to Kal-El (Superman's Kryptonian name)—which was, coincidentally, the same time that the boys' pants became too short and their knees grew knobby—I brought home Superman tooth-brushes, and Ford and Owen told me they wanted Batman.

Excuse me?

And just like that, a piece of their childhood was gone.

I folded Ford's and Owen's old Superman shirts and tucked them away in their new baby brother's drawer. The familiar yellow emblems on the front were cracked and faded. There were holes in the armpits. I sat down on the floor and laughed. I could still so plainly see Ford and Owen running through the front yard, capes horizontal with the ground, on their way to save the day, or the dog, whichever. I cried holding one of the soft cotton shirts to my chest. When my husband came into the room, he said, "My gosh, you'll be a mess when they go off to college some day."

Everyone said this would happen. Old ladies at the mall used to hang over the stroller and tell me, "They grow up so fast, just you wait!" My mom said, "Before you know it, they'll be all grown up." Ford and Owen aren't there yet, but for the first time I'm beginning to see what everyone tried to tell me: time goes by faster than . . . well, faster than a speeding bullet. It seemed like just yesterday that I lived with two little Supermen. Eventually, today will seem like yesterday, too.

After our third son was born this January, the doctor said to me, "Well, I guess you know what to do with this one." And I do: I'll start him on Superman early, I'll take more pictures, I'll worry less, and I'll enjoy more. Because I know one day—far too soon—I'll bring home a Superman toothbrush, and it will be the wrong one.

Sarah Smiley

One More Moment

Only moments ago loud, panting gasps and a crescendo of moans crowded the air itself out of the room. But now there was only calm. Hush. Tranquility. Even my racing heart grew still. I swiped a forearm across my damp brow, reluctant to shift my eyes—for even a second—from the bundle I was cradling.

Already, the pain and exhaustion are a distant memory. I was too busy marveling at the miracle of new life to concern myself with the midwife's final ministrations. Like Alice through the looking glass, I had stepped into another world. A world of wonder. A world of possibility.

With a curious fingertip, I traced her ear, as delicate as a seashell, then her wisp of a brow, and trailed lazily lower to her ducky-down cheek. I loosened the swaddling to inspect translucent nails and rosebud toes and to count them. One at a time.

I smoothed her cotton-ball head, and sipped at her puckered lips, content to simply watch her breathe. In and out, in and out, in and out. The tiny movement of her chest was barely perceptible. My breath caught when she opened her eyes and gazed into mine for a long, sacred moment. Satisfied, I hoped, with what they've seen, they feathered closed again.

I gathered her closer, rag-doll limp, surprising myself at the sudden, fierce rush of proprietorship and protectiveness I felt when the nurse reached to take her from my arms. *No, just a bit longer.* I nestled her closer, under my chin, near my heart.

I stroked a loose fold in her skin, knowing she would grow into it as surely as I was to fill my new calling. Even so, doubt wagged its head and I wondered, *Am I ready for this unexplored role and the job description that comes with it? Can I give this baby the important and best parts of myself?*

I squeezed my eyes against the threat of tears. *There's been more than one birth here this day,* I finally realized. And then, reluctantly, I leaned over the bed to hand this precious first grandbaby back into the impatient, outstretched arms of my daughter.

Carol McAdoo Rehme

In Concert with Mom

M usic *is well said to be the speech of angels.*

Thomas Carlyle

When my oldest son was in high school, he planned to attend a Christian contemporary concert with the youth group from our church. To my amazement, Aaron invited me to go along; he knew I enjoyed the music of one of the performers. I readily accepted; however, by the time the date of the concert arrived, I had questions about going. My youngest son, who has Down syndrome and progressive heart disease, had been ill, and I was concerned about him. My husband encouraged me to attend the concert, assuring me he was quite capable of taking care of our youngest. I wavered.

Finally, it hit me. Aaron was sixteen years old. How many opportunities would I have to do something fun with him before he went away to college? And how many youth actually invited their mothers to attend a concert with them that was clearly geared for teens? The decision was made. I would not miss this opportunity.

At the concert, I sat with Aaron and his girlfriend in the

third row, stuffing cotton in my ears to block out the loud, ear-splitting amplified music of the first performer. I stood when the kids stood, clapped when they clapped, and never let anyone know how nervous I was to feel the floor vibrate beneath my feet. Aaron and his friends were amused at my enthusiasm.

By the time we left the concert, I was certain my hearing was damaged forever. My ears were ringing and sounds seemed muffled, but it quickly passed. So did my son's teenage years. In no time he was in college and away from home. I missed him more than I could say. On days when I was especially lonely for his ready smile and his teasing manner, I would think back to the concert we attended and be thankful once again that I didn't pass up an opportunity to spend time with my son.

Aaron is now grown and has a family of his own, but we are still very close. Some days he calls just to chat and tell me about his day. I drop everything and enjoy the moment, knowing these times too shall pass.

We sometimes reminisce on that concert of years ago when my teenage son and I made a lifetime memory. Aaron always laughs about the fact that his mom was the "only" person in the whole youth group to get an autograph from the performer.

Louise Tucker Jones

With All My Love

The tricycle tipped my three-year-old granddaughter onto the sidewalk before I could buffer her fall. Emily lay there for a moment, calculating her chances of survival. Figuring the odds were in her favor, she sat up with a smile that quickly turned into tears when she saw the blood on her knee. I scooped her up, cooing words of comfort as I carried her into the house to mend her hurt.

With much reassuring and the universally accepted Grandma cookie bribe, she let me wash and put ointment on her scrape. We searched through the band-aid box until Emily found a neon pink one to wear as a badge on her boo-boo.

I kissed her cheek. "All better now, sweetie?"

"No, Gamma, you hafta say the Mommy words," she said. I quickly ran a list of Mommy words through my mind: *Please? Thank you? I love you?* "You know, Gamma. Mommy says them to make me all better." Emily took a deep breath and recited, "A little kiss, a little hug, I give you these, with all my love."

My heart swirled and remembered. It was the same little ditty that I had said to my children, my mother to me, and her mother to her. My grandmother had died when my mother was eight. There had been no silverware, no china, no jewelry to inherit, nothing to hold but her dear memories. When she became a mother herself, she passed on the gentle love of her mother and the remembered comfort of the "Mommy words" that made all bad things go away and only the good remain. Hearing it now, I realized that though I had never met my grandmother, I did know her. We were mothers—we were connected at the heart

"Don't cry, Gamma. I be all better."

Emily and I kissed and hugged, and said the Mommy words to each other. I heard my grandmother's, my mother's, my daughter's, my granddaughter's, and my own voice blending through time. It was as though my grandmother had written her legacy of love on the hearts of four generations of mothers and then signed it;

A little kiss, a little hug, I give you these, with all my love.

Cynthia Hamond

"How long did you intern with Grandma
before you became a full-fledged Mom?"

The Autumn Leaves of Summer

We must accept finite disappointment, but never lose infinite hope.

Martin Luther King Jr.

Trouble began brewing right at the start of summer vacation, precisely when my grandmother gave Mom that hideous bolt of fabric. My mother couldn't sew a stitch, and my grandmother spent the bulk of her retirement in a fruitless effort to reverse this quirk of fate. While my grandmother could turn a flour sack into a party frock in an afternoon, and fashion a lace-trimmed hanky out of the scraps, the most my mother could do with the same flour sack is turn it into a decorative trash can liner—maybe.

Though creating a fashion statement consistently eluded Mom's skill, it never once escaped her desire. From that ugly bolt of fabric scattered with autumn leaves sprang the grandiose idea that Mom would whip up matching summer tops for my three sisters and me.

Undaunted by the absence of talent, Mom once again forged ahead with boundless enthusiasm. Her energy grew in direct proportion to my paranoia as I imagined us venturing down the street in leafy looking halter-tops, pitching apples at passersby like the grumpy trees in the *Wizard of Oz*.

So I suggested a tablecloth might be just the perfect idea. "Mom, can't you just see our dining room table come Thanksgiving? Picture that plump juicy turkey with all the trimmings, arranged just so on a spray of autumn leaves. If word of this gets out, *Better Homes and Gardens* will be beating down your door for a photo shoot."

Who was I kidding? This was one hopeless situation. Or was it? My mom's projects usually rode a one-way ticket from the sewing machine to the rag sack with no stops inbetween, and that was no secret. Her unbroken string of sewing catastrophes fostered strong hope in me. It was a tentative smile I wore, but ever so smug just the same.

With fabric in hand, mother disappeared into the basement and headed down those same steps every night thereafter. The muffled hum of the Singer motor rising up through the floorboards slowly wiped the smug smile from my face and replaced it with the trembling lip of an obsessive adolescent helplessly drowning in a pool of self-inflicted fear of embarrassment. I just knew those autumn leaves, bathed in my mother's best intentions, were waiting in the wings . . . and not in the form of any Thanksgiving tablecloth.

True to my prediction, Mom emerged from the basement one evening with outstretched arms draped in yards, and yards, and yards of autumn leaves. Forget the trembling lip. By now I was picking out the bridge from which I intended to fling myself into everlasting eternity.

"Eeewww, Mom. What are they? Awnings?" my charming brother asked.

"They're summer tops," she said. "I made them for your sisters. Pretty good, huh? I didn't even have a pattern!"

One glance brought that harsh reality to life with a

vengeance. Imagine, if you will, two bandanna handkerchiefs placed on top of each other—that's what my mother did with two squares of fabric. She stitched straight across the top of each "garment," leaving a huge gaping hole in the center for our heads to fit through without the aid of a single button, snap, or zipper. Mom didn't have a clue about sewing notions. In the same wide-open style, two giant armholes flanked either side of the neckline. And, she accomplished all of this without the use of darts, pleats, tucks, or so much as a trace amount of elastic.

"Oh boy! Mom. They're terrific!" I said, desperately trying to sound sincere. I don't think I had ever seen her look so proud. To make matters worse, she bought us matching brown shorts and labeled these atrocities our "special occasion outfits."

Day after blissful day passed without a single special occasion in sight, until the day of doom when the invitation to our cousin's wedding shower arrived. Shrouded in a cloud of "special occasion" gloom, my three sisters and I prepared for the worst.

As expected, Mom insisted we break out the tree suits and inflict on an unsuspecting world, the most unhappy group of sisters you ever saw, sporting a wardrobe of fall foliage in the middle of a record breaking heat wave.

After dressing on the day of the shower, my sisters and I formed a small circle between two matching sets of bunk beds in the room we all shared. We stood there, staring at each other in disbelief. Clad in shades of Irish-setter red and butterscotch yellow, set off by remarkably ugly brown shorts, we looked like poster children for Arbor Day.

At the height of our pity party, my oldest sister started laughing uncontrollably, which set off a chain reaction. In the throws of our laughter, Mom's love had penetrated that scratchy old fabric and snuggled softly around us.

I can still see her proud smile as she watched us pile out of the car and line up on the sidewalk, wearing her hand-made works of art. We proudly escorted our mother up the front path and joined in the fun. Whether the other party guests were laughing with us, or at us, remains a mystery I have no desire to solve.

It's true; Mom never did create a fashion statement, unless you consider the countless memories she lovingly stitched into our hearts with unyielding joy. That alone qualifies my mom as a most remarkable seamstress.

Annmarie B. Tait

If Floors Could Talk

No act of kindness, no matter how small, is ever wasted.

Aesop

My bedroom floor—in the house I grew up in—holds a deep, dark secret. It lay hidden for many years, away from those who might cause repercussions if it was revealed. I know the secret came to light a few years ago, but by then no one who cared was around to witness it. For all that time my mother and I were the keepers of the secret.

I was about seventeen and a bit of a wannabe hippie. I gravitated toward the unusual. I don't know where my decorating scheme came from, but it was pretty far out there. The strange thing was that my mother agreed to it. I thought she was pretty cool—most of my friends wouldn't be allowed to have a room like mine. I'm fairly certain their mothers wouldn't have helped them, but mine did despite the fact she was very picky about her house.

My mother, sister, and I painted two walls bright purple, one brilliant yellow, and the last with a purple and yellow sunrise. I remember our foray into tie-dyeing like it was yesterday. On a mellow fall afternoon canopied with an azure sky, Mother lugged huge pots of water outdoors. We poured in packets of dye, wrapped rubber bands around sheets, and twisted and dipped to create purple and yellow bedspread, sheets, and curtains.

I finished off the room with posters and some huge yellow and purple acrylic flowers in Mexican pots. Mother bought a light box to hook up to the stereo that produced multicolored, pulsating light in time to the music. What a mother—June Cleaver and Gloria Steinem rolled into one.

I still had a few finishing touches, but I could accomplish them on my own. One night I was in my room with the door closed so as not to awaken my daddy, who had an early bedtime because of his job. I had the music going and was really in the groove of things. I spread some newspaper on the hardwood floor and began to paint some bottles with crystallizing paint. I had a yellow one finished and set aside so I opened the purple paint and reached for the bottle. Somehow, I bumped the can the wrong way and over it went—beyond the newspaper. Need I mention that my mother kept those hardwood floors waxed to perfection? June Cleaver—remember?

"Oh, no. I'm dead." I froze in horror as the purple puddle spread and grew larger than a dinner plate. I finally thawed enough to grab some newspaper and swipe at the puddle. Most of the paint came up but the stain remained. "Aaaah!" I screamed silently.

No way was I waking Daddy up. I skulked past his bedroom and headed for the den where my mother was watching television. "Mother, I spilled the paint and wiped it up, but it didn't come up, and there's such a mess." My words tumbled over each other in my panic.

My mother was a quick woman, especially when the catastrophe concerned her children and house. She made it to my room faster than a speeding bullet, took one look at the mess, and bolted for a wet, soapy rag. She washed and scrubbed without saying a word. The purple faded the tiniest bit.

"Mother, I'm so sorry. I didn't mean to do it. The paint just tipped over." I was so upset my entire body trembled.

She placed a calming hand on my arm. "I know you didn't do it on purpose."

"Daddy's going to kill me."

"Let me get something else." She went to the kitchen for a different cleanser.

I hunched over the stain, willing it to disappear. If I had known Shakespeare's famous words regarding "a spot," I probably would have chanted them. She tried a few more things that didn't work. By this time I was crying. "Daddy's going to be so mad."

She comforted me again. "Everything will be all right."

There was nothing to do but go to bed and wait for the morning and my reckoning with Daddy. The telltale stain glowed all night in the moonbeams shining through the window. Like Lady Macbeth, my sleep was troubled by the treacherous stain that wouldn't go away. My mother knew the truth. Would she incriminate me? Morning finally came and miraculously, a summons didn't appear. Instead, my mother came home from a shopping trip with a nice area rug for my bedroom.

Years after I grew up and moved away, they installed wall-to-wall carpeting. To my knowledge, up to his passing away in 2002, Daddy never knew about the stain. Mother sold the house a few years ago. The buyer told her they were taking up the carpet and going back to the hardwood floors.

When she told me this, I said, "They're going to have a surprise under the carpet in my bedroom."

"I had forgotten all about that," she answered.

Daddy never knew and Mother had forgotten, but I would never forget the symbol of forgiveness from the bottom of my mother's heart.

Sandra McGarrity

"My friends voted you best mom in town,
for letting us hang out here . . . and
for providing the widest variety of snacks!"

Instrument of Love

You can't change the music of your soul.

Katharine Hepburn

"Hurry and finish breakfast, honey. We have some new music to learn today."

The sun was barely up, yet here we sat upon the piano bench, mother and daughter, welcoming the new day in song.

"Finger three goes on G," I gently instructed. "Are your fingers curved and in good position?"

Blue eyes rolled under her wire-framed glasses. Seven-year-old Emily sighed before repeating the measure, adding a little "forte" to emphasize that this time she did, indeed, hit the correct note.

Careful not to be too hard on her. Stress the positive and make it fun, I reminded myself. "That was much better!"

Reminiscing, I thought back to my own mother, thirty years ago, sitting beside me as I practiced scales and sonatinas before sunrise. Her pink satin slippers peeking out from under her bathrobe, Mom sipped steaming coffee while guiding me through my lesson books. We were six-thirty people, meeting at the crack of dawn each day, like clockwork. ("It's best if you get your practicing out of the way before school," was Mom's adage.) Despite working a second-shift job and getting six hours of sleep, Mom never missed a practice session. "That was nice. How about trying it one more time?" she would say to me.

Mom's instruction was always subtle, her gentle manner filling me with love. Her coaching was about life: "Practice every day. Always try your best." And the knowledge that I didn't even fully realize until thirty years later: "Spend quality time with your daughter. Be there for her no matter what."

Sliding across the piano bench, I gave Emily a hug. We played duets and alouettes; not perfectly at first, but eventually with some semblance of harmony and rhythm. "Let's play it again, Mom!" Em's eyes, the same pair that were rolling with frustration just twenty minutes earlier, were now brimming with the glow of accomplishment. I, too, felt a sort of glow . . . a love between generations cemented years earlier, on a piano bench in the early light of day.

"Mom, you should have heard her play at the recital! She didn't miss a note!" It was a week later, and I felt the need to brag about my musician. I knew exactly who to call first.

"Well of course she did a great job! You tell Em that Grandma is proud of her. And don't forget to give her a big, sweet kiss."

Hanging up the phone, I walked into my bedroom, checking that the alarm was set for the next morning. We are, as we always have been, six-thirty people, mother and daughter, playing our instrument of love.

Stefanie Wass

Of Lizards and Laughter and Love

Laughter is the shortest distance between two people.

Victor Borge

My first-born was a "boundary banger." Whatever boundary his dad and I established for Josh, he hit it as hard as he could—testing to see if he could push past our parental limits. Josh challenged bedtimes, television restrictions, and even having to wear a coat during the winter. When I told him not to run, he said, "I'm just walking fast." If I told him it was time to get out of the pool, he conveniently dunked his head underwater and didn't hear me.

By the time Josh was nine years old, I was just as tired of saying "Don't" as Josh was of hearing it. There were days I felt like a human boundary line, worn out by my son's insistent defiance. I wanted fewer power struggles and more fun with my strong-willed son. I longed for memories echoing with shared laughter, not just the sound of my voice repeating, "No. No. No."

Rather than being on opposing teams about what Josh

could do or not do, I devised a challenge we could enjoy
together. And so, I bought a green-and-orange plastic
lizard. My game plan was simple: I would hide "Lizard"
and dare Josh to find it.

My first attempt was easy. I snuggled its three-inch,
striped plastic form into Josh's tennis shoe. I chuckled as I
imagined him finding it when he got dressed for school
the next morning. Sure enough, he came into the kitchen,
Lizard dangling from his hand and a bemused "What's
going on, Mom?" look on his face.

"Good job! You found him. Now, you hide Lizard and I'll
find him." With a grin, Josh picked up the gauntlet—I
mean, Lizard—already plotting the perfect hiding place.

And so it began. I found Lizard under my pillow, nestled among my shampoo and conditioner bottles in the
shower, and between my car visors. Once, I picked up my
water bottle to find Lizard floating among the ice cubes.
Another time, I crawled into bed, rolled over on my back,
and saw Lizard leering at me from the light fixture on my
ceiling fan. Josh's most memorable attempt? Positioning
Lizard under the toilet lid. That was quite an unexpected—and uncomfortable—discovery during my
middle-of-the-night bathroom visit.

When it was my turn, I tucked Lizard in Josh's book bag,
in the refrigerator among the leftovers, behind the couch
pillows, and in his coat pocket.

Sometimes a hiding place was too good and Lizard lan-
guished unfound for months. We misplaced Lizard a few
times through the years, but I only had to replace him
once. Josh hid Lizard too well, and I was stumped. It was
only after we'd moved from Florida to Colorado that I
found Lizard as I unpacked a box full of household odds
and ends.

Hiding Lizard was more than just a game. It was a silly
but concrete way of showing Josh that I loved him—and

for him to show me he loved me. Whenever I discovered Lizard nestled in my sock drawer or lurking in my washing machine, I imagined Josh plotting the ideal hiding place and then anticipating me finding it. Whenever Josh found Lizard lounging in his cereal bowl or resting on a bar of soap in the tub, he knew I was thinking about him. An inexpensive rubber reptile became a tangible expression of love between us.

As Josh grew up, our game of reptile hide-and-seek was sometimes forgotten for months at a time. But when then-fourteen-year-old Josh packed for a nine-week mission trip to Kenya, I smuggled Lizard into his duffel bag. When he moved into his college dorm, I packaged Lizard and mailed him to Josh.

When Josh got married this past May, I made good on my promise that Lizard would go along on his honeymoon. Since I once again couldn't find Lizard, a friend donated one of her boys' toy lizards to the cause. We made up a gift basket filled with a bottle of champagne and chocolate and other goodies that was delivered to Josh and Jenelle's hotel room. The lizard lounged in a champagne glass.

As Josh and his bride left for their honeymoon, I smiled to myself, knowing I'd ultimately bested my son in our longstanding game. An hour later, I walked out to my car, happily exhausted from celebrating with family and friends. I slid into the driver's seat, and there, perched on my dashboard, was a tiny brown-and-yellow striped plastic lizard. I put my head down on my steering wheel and laughed as I cried.

My son sure hates to lose—and that's one of the things I love about him.

Beth K. Vogt

Milestones

Milestones are those things you're supposed to see coming from a long way off and be prepared for. My youngest child started first grade this week, which was a milestone I thought I was eager to reach. For sixteen years, I've been an at-home mom.

I clearly remember a day when I was nursing a baby, while making a toddler a sandwich, and trying to talk a frightened five-year-old down from the top bunk of his new bed. I felt exhausted and overwhelmed. "If only I had some time to myself," I wailed to a friend.

"Cindy, someday you'll blink, and all the boys will be in school. Then you'll have your time," she said.

I must have blinked.

I wouldn't trade my time at home with my sons for anything. I understand how fortunate I've been to have had this choice. The sacrifices my husband and I have made have been worth it.

However, there were days I couldn't recall why I ever wanted to have children to begin with, much less be with them 24/7. There were weeks I envied the working moms on my block with their shiny briefcases, flawless makeup, and lunches at places other than Chuck E. Cheese.

Months in which I longed to send my toddler off to school, preferably boarding school.

For years I fantasized about what I'd do when all the boys were in school. I dreamed of buying clothes with tags that said, "Dry Clean Only," and longed for the time when I'd be able to finish a thought or a sentence. "Some day I'll have a bigger life," I'd say.

But bigger is not always better, and I found myself at the door of Sam's classroom, unable to walk away. I'm not much of a crier, probably because I live with five guys, but my eyes grew suspiciously moist. Sam looked up and waved, as if to say, "You can go now." Suddenly, I wasn't sure if I was ready to leave him or have him leave me.

I know I'm not done parenting by any means. My teenagers don't need me to cut the crusts of their sandwiches or help them blow their noses, but I'm still their chauffeur, calendar-keeper, and when they choose to speak, a listening ear. It's time for me to embrace a new season of life, to reengage in a world that doesn't revolve around snacks and naps.

This is my time—finally. I took one last peek at Sam, busily coloring at his desk. Slowly, I closed the door to his first-grade classroom. I patted my briefcase and checked my lipstick.

Milestones are often bittersweet. As I open the door to this new season of my life, I choose to savor the sweet portions and leave the bitterness behind.

Cindy Hval

2

A MOTHER'S GUIDING HAND

A mother's heart is the child's schoolroom

Henry Ward Beecher

Bearing Gifts from Afar

*Those who bring sunshine to the lives of others
cannot keep it from themselves.*

James Barrie

It was nearly midnight when I pulled into a parking
space at the rear of the hospital. We entered the emergency room, and a feeling of déjà vu washed over me. The
ER was sadly crowded to standing room only. Eyes filled
with pain and exhaustion swung in our direction as we
stepped up to the security window.

"We're going to the NICU," I said, which stands for
Neonatal Intensive Care Unit. I pronounced it "nick-you."

The security guard looked at me askance, perhaps wondering what a mother with two preteen boys was doing
up at this ungodly hour.

"My boys here used to be residents of the NICU," I said,
chuckling over his puzzled expression. "A long, long time
ago."

Striding through the maze of hallways in search of an
elevator, I felt the warm embrace of memories. Eleven
years ago my husband and I had walked these gleaming
linoleum corridors at all hours of the day and night to visit

Cody, the first of our three preemies. Cody was born at twenty-four weeks during the week of Christmas and could fit in a velvet-lined stocking. Ten months later, we welcomed Ethan, whose premature arrival meant premature lungs. He stayed in the NICU for ten days until he could breathe on his own. The same happened to Matthew, our eight-year-old, whose premature lungs required a seventeen-day stay in the NICU.

Being a NICU momma, I witnessed my share of traumatic episodes, but even more so the brilliant rays of hope among noisy machines, oxygen tubes, crash carts, loud mail chutes, and donated rocking chairs. As tired, anxious parents in thin, cotton gowns, we did everything we could to ease the pain of our little miracles. We draped baby blankets over incubators to shield them from harsh lighting. We kangarooed our babies to bring their blood pressure down. We learned to cup their heads with our hands to mimic the snugness of the womb. We softly sang lullabies and whispered prayers.

Our most cherished keepsakes from our time in the NICU were from anonymous Samaritans. Church ladies sewed tiny blankets and teeny one-piece gowns that could fit Cody. Others made plastic ball ornaments, inside of which floated a photo of my son in a cushion of brightly colored confetti. Still others left holiday notes, cards, and mementos at the stations where each of my sons recuperated.

I snapped back to the present. We stood in the foyer outside the NICU. I pointed to the deep sink with the soap pump. Metal shelves next to the sink held stacks of neatly folded, colorful hospital gowns. "Dad and I would wash up and pick out a gown to wear before going into the NICU to visit you guys."

"Wow!" my boys said in their hushed library voices.

I stepped in front of the camera to the right of the door and pressed the buzzer.

"Yes?" a female voice called from inside.

I told her the Oliver family was here to drop off the gifts.

"Oh, yes! I'll be out in a sec."

As the door swung open, a nurse stepped out along with a smiling gown-clad couple. The couple huddled over one of those cell phones that took photos.

They were obviously admiring a picture they had just captured of their little one. Back in "my day" we had no such new-fangled technology.

I introduced my NICU veterans to the nurse. "This is my oldest, Cody. He was here in 1994 and weighed 1 pound, 6 ounces. Then his brother here, Ethan, was born a month early. I wanted to show them where their first home was."

Cody and Ethan peeked with wide eyes through the crack of the door as I handed the plastic bags to the nurse.

"Oh, these look beautiful!" she said. "I know the mothers will really be surprised. Thank you so much!"

Earlier that evening at our kitchen table, Cody and Ethan had worked diligently on their "Good Turn" project. As part of meeting their Webelos requirements in Cub Scouts, they assembled angel necklaces. They strung satin ribbons through large Ideal Clamps (a metal paperclip resembling the body of an angel) and on each one threaded a bead onto the ribbon until the bead resembled the angel's head between the "wings" of the paperclip. They tied a knot at the other end, and voila . . . an angel necklace.

After they assembled thirty-plus necklaces—some in navy blue, others in polka-dotted pink, still others in lavender, white, and forest green—I folded them carefully inside gallon-sized plastic bags, and together the three of us made the forty-five-minute commute to the hospital.

"I hope the mothers like our necklaces!" Ethan said as we walked back to our car behind the hospital. The pale moon was our witness at this witching hour.

"Oh, I know they will, sweetie," I answered, my eyes misting. "More than you'll ever know."

The following day would be Mother's Day. While the NICU mothers will be surprised by angel necklaces lovingly created by NICU veterans, this mother will be thanking God for all the nameless Samaritans and their day-brightening treasures left at each of my sons' stations.

Jennifer Oliver

On My Side

The best proof of love is trust.

Joyce Brothers

A fellow second-grader had told the teacher that I had taken coins from the March of Dimes canister. This wasn't true.

The can had been placed on Mrs. Christiansen's desk so all the kids could contribute dimes to try to cure the terrible polio that had made so many people, mostly children, unable to walk. Our President Roosevelt himself spent much time in a wheelchair and on crutches as a result of this disease.

It was true that I had put my hand into the can, so I could keep track of the coins I was counting with my finger. I hadn't taken any dimes out of the can as my classmate had reported, and even though I told Mrs. Christiansen this, she called my mother anyway.

When all the kids left after school, Mrs. Christiansen, my mother, and I remained in the classroom. My mother sat down at one of the little desks across from me, but her long legs wouldn't fit and they reached all the way across the aisle and ended up under my desk. She looked into my eyes and we held hands.

"Mrs. Christiansen tells me that someone saw you put your hand in the March of Dimes can. I will only ask you one time, and you only have to answer one time," my mother said to me. "Jackie, did you take any of the dimes?"

"No, Mama," I answered.

She kept holding my hand as went up to Mrs. Christiansen's desk.

"Jackie didn't take any dimes. Now we're going to Borden's for ice cream.

From that moment, I knew my mother would always stand up for me, and I knew I would always tell her the truth . . . forever.

Jackie Fleming

A Mother's Gifts

What can I give to you, Daughter dear,
My baby, so fragile and small?
Only your love and your care, Mother,
For a mother's love conquers all.

What can I do for you now, Daughter,
Now you're a young girl in school?
Make sure I learn all my lessons, Mother,
For I'd rather be nobody's fool!

What can I give as a gift, Daughter,
Now you're to be a man's wife?
Give me support and advice, Mother,
But allow me to live my own life.

How can I help you the most, Daughter,
Now you're a mother-to-be?
With my children share laughter and wisdom, Mother.
Tell them what it means to be free.

What can I give you of mine, Daughter,
Now I'm old, to show you I cared?
Only a kiss, with your blessing, Mother,
And the memories of good times we shared.

I wish I had given you more, Daughter,
But our time here on earth is too short.
You taught me all life is a gift, Mother,
And the things we prize most are not bought.

Valerie J. Palmer

A Common Thread

The three-ply cord is not easily severed.

Ecclesiastes 4:12

I'm not sure how the tradition originated. Either it was pure financial necessity due to my father being in medical school, or perhaps my mother's desire to be unique by creating homemade clothing. Whatever the reason, her outfits were clearly labors of love.

Each homemade outfit was carefully thought out, whether the ideas came from well-worn pattern books or the latest American import (we lived in South Africa). Investing hours of time and energy, she painstakingly cut out and measured, pinned, and stitched each individual creation. While matching mother-daughter outfits was the latest rage in the United States, they were unheard of in my country in the early 1970s. Each new season would herald small versions for me, larger for herself. Pastel pinks or party polka dots, cotton or corduroy, each outfit would be worn with a sense of pride, as people would stop to compliment my mother on both the original clothes as well as "that pretty little daughter who looks just like you!"

Skinny as a rail with long sticklike arms and legs, I would glow with pleasure as I realized that the magic outfits had tricked everyone into believing that I mirrored my beautiful mother. I would stand a little straighter, practice smiling the same way she did, and began to believe that some day I, too, might be as comely and clever.

As the years passed and I entered the turbulent, traumatic teens, our relationship changed. My moodiness seemed mirrored in her face, and my fluctuating needs and emotions made it difficult enough for me to live with myself, never mind with anyone else. Whatever she said, I did the opposite. If she liked an outfit, I automatically hated it. If she approved, I automatically disapproved.

In defense and in hindsight, I now realize I was no different than most adolescents in the never-ending quest for balance, both physically and emotionally. I think that one of the most benevolent blessings God encoded in human genetics is the all-encompassing love of parents for their offspring. While we may not always like the actions, or even character, of our children, that inner love is always present. Perhaps this love alone is what leaves the door to our hearts ajar, regardless of how often the door to our homes may be slammed shut. Eventually time and maturity soothed my unrest, and I grew into what I hope can be termed an "adult."

A generation later, Mom's clothing tradition continues. Now it is my turn to search the pattern books and ponder over materials. For my first attempt, I made matching skirts for my little daughter and me. Once again proving her creativity, my mother changed hobbies—completing our ensemble by knitting matching sweaters for us. Each time we wear them, my daughter begs me to go for a walk around the neighborhood with her, and makes sure it's during a time when everyone is outside. The look in her eyes and the glow on her cheeks bring back memories, as she too basks in the feeling of security created by the knowledge that she is an important and beloved member of our family.

Perhaps some day we'll make Grandma/Mother/Daughter ensembles, and it will be proof that love and traditions connect the generations.

Michelle Borinstein

A Mother First

My mother did not work outside the home until later in life. And then she worked part-time in a bakery, waiting on people. She had me play where she could see me from the window, and often I would run inside to get a treat. At the time, she believed only her eyes were good enough to ensure my safety. She was always a mother first.

It was apparent to me, even at a young age, that wearing the title "mom" was my mother's most important identity. I felt it in the way she looked at me, in her voice, and in her touch. From the beginning, almost to a fault, my mother offered me the most important part of her besides her love—her attention. In spite of the problems tossed her way, the distractions, her own yearnings for more in her marriage and in her life, she at least had attained one goal—to be a mother first.

Sometimes she would go overboard with her enthusiasm. If it was cold, I had on too many sweaters and never could be without my earmuffs. If it was hot, and our apartment was always hot, she would flee to the beaches and hurry me into the ocean. She was a worrying mother, and when a famous family lost their child in a kidnapping, my mother put bottles of coins on the window ledge so that, if they fell, she would be warned there was an intruder in the house. And if anyone threatened me at school with a schoolyard confrontation, my mother would square off with them if she found out. She was my protector, supporter, and the first person who ever made me feel as if I were special, as nowhere else in life.

I can still hear her voice encouraging me on my first date. "Go," she ordered. "Have fun," she smiled. "And don't let him touch you," she warned. And when I was older, and a date had left me waiting while he went out on the boardwalk with someone else, my mother found him and later told me, "I gave him a piece of my mind." Though mortified at the time by her behavior, it is a memory I cherish.

Later in life, I wondered how she could know so much about me that I did not know about myself. She knew even though my marks were average in school, that I was just bored but smart enough. She believed in me even when I made mistakes that caused others to shudder. She wanted me to be more than she had been, when I thought she was everything I wanted to be.

Recently my children—a son and daughter—came to visit. In their forties now, they are married and with children of their own. Both were tired and soon fell asleep, one on the couch, the other on the bed. Carefully, while they slept, I took some blankets and tucked them in, as I had done so many times when they were young. I took the telephone off the receiver, so they would not be disturbed, lowered the shades, and for a precious moment, watched over them, grateful to be, just as my mother had been, a mother first.

Harriet May Savitz

Take Me Out to the Ballgame

It's déjà vu all over again!

Yogi Berra

The two-hour car ride seemed to take days as we passed cornfields, bean fields, and soon, as we approached the city, very modern-looking buildings. The excitement was growing as we passed each milepost. My father and I were taking my young son to his first major league ballgame in Chicago.

With this trip, we were creating a new generational tradition; my father took me as a young child, and today, we were both going to open a new world to my young son. At age five, he loved baseball. He didn't quite understand the concept of what he was about to experience, nor did I until I was there.

To pass the time in the car, his grandfather and I filled his mind with historical facts that he would understand. We told him how Babe Ruth, supposedly, called his home run shot at Wrigley Field. We told him stories of great Cub players, such as Ryne Sandberg, Ernie Banks, Ron Santo, and Billy Williams.

Once we made it to the city, his eyes were filled with amazement! Coming from a very small town literally in the middle of a cornfield, this was a whole new world to him. There was so much to see! He was in awe at the trains and the buildings, and as we neared the airport, he couldn't believe his eyes at how big the airplanes were and how close to the ground they flew.

Finally, we reached our destination. As we rounded the corner, there it stood: Wrigley Field. The bricks seemed to open up and swallow us into a whole different world—the sea of blue and white shirts, the vendors all trying to sell us their scorecards, T-shirts, Cracker Jacks, and anything else under the sun they could possibly market.

I looked down at my son, and his eyes were the size of the baseballs he loves to play with. I giggled because while there was so much to look at and so much to take in, I knew we had just begun the whole experience. So before we entered the park itself, we walked around the entire perimeter of the park. He saw the outside view of the old towering scoreboard. The flags on top of the scoreboard were gently flowing out toward us, which any Cub fan would know is a huge factor in the outcome of the game; the "Wrigley Winds" determined a lot of how the game was to be played that day. With the wind blowing out of the park, the ball would be, too!

We walked by the firehouse right across the street and peeked in. The firemen, when not on a call, will sit on their lawn chairs right outside the firehouse and take in the sights and sounds that surround the beautiful field. We walked back to show him where the players park. He picked out a black Hummer as his favorite, which we believe belongs to Carlos Zambrano, his favorite pitcher. "I wonder what Sammy drives, Mommy." I was thrilled to hear the magic taking over in his eyes and voice.

We finally made it around to the gates to enter the park.

The lines were long but moved quickly. Once inside the concourse, the excitement grew for all of us, and the smell of hot dogs and popcorn filled our noses. With a firm grip on his tiny hand, we carefully looked for the sign to point us to our seats. We walked under the banners that hung from the ceiling honoring many of our "Boys in Blue" from the past. I stopped briefly to take a picture of the banner of my favorite player, Ryne Sandberg. He was the starting second baseman the day my dad first brought me to Wrigley Field and is now in the MLB Hall of Fame.

We finally found our section—Section 220. This was the moment I knew my son would remember for the rest of his life. We slowly walked up the concrete stairs and as we reached the top step, there she was. It felt as if someone had unveiled the most beautiful piece of artwork— Wrigley Field. The green ivy against the red bricks seemed greener than I remembered. The green grass was cut in a pattern that made it look painted. The huge green scoreboard across the field from us towered over the tiny little people out in the bleachers. The sign scrolling across the bottom said, "Welcome to Wrigley Field." The organ was playing an upbeat version of "It's A Beautiful Day for a Ballgame." I looked down at my son—he was frozen, with a look on his face as if it were Christmas morning.

My father and I pulled him to our seats, but he wouldn't sit. He was too busy taking it all in as the players were down on the field warming up. "Look, Mom! Number 21! That's Sammy Sosa! Mom, that's Sammy Sosa, right there!" His excitement nearly brought me to tears. I had just created a die-hard Cub fan right before my eyes. I had just passed down one of my passions to my son, a passion that I received from the man sitting on the other side of me, my dad. What a moment!

Heather McAlvey

The Velvet Tradition

We are all like one-winged angels. It's only when we help each other that we can fly.

Luciano de Crescendo

"Mom, help, the Christmas pageant is tonight! Emily just gave me the note this morning. She had left it in her desk," cried my daughter Jen frantically. "Can you meet me somewhere down the coast and bring the coat?"

"Of course," I replied. The thought of driving in the heavy morning traffic of the Christmas season was not pleasant, but we agreed to meet in exactly two hours.

As I drove along, I thought of our conversation just weeks before. Jen had come over to celebrate her daughter Emily's sixth birthday. That evening I had taken her into the bedroom and carefully pulled the black velvet coat out of the trunk. Her eyes had lit up, "You still have that coat Grandma made! I remember I wore it for Christmas when I was seven."

"Yes," I said. "It's still a beauty, considering it's age, and I want Emily to wear it for her Christmas play." I opened the coat to show her the detail work on the white quilted lining and let her feel the heaviness of the real velvet. "Your grandmother was a wonderful seamstress," I beamed.

I was amazed how proud I was of my mom's work, considering the fact I had never really appreciated it until now. She had made all my clothes. I was dressed in ruffles and frills as far back as I could recall. When I got my first job, I told her I was going to a boutique to buy my clothes. I'll never forget the hurt look on her face.

But time marched on, and my mother was thrilled when I presented her with a granddaughter. She loved babies and started sewing again. Her trusty Singer came out of storage and the ruffles and frills flew through her hands— dresses, jumpers, pantsuits, and aprons.

As I drove, I thought of how touched my mother would be to see that I had passed one of her prized creations on to her great-granddaughter.

I pulled into the huge service station right on time, and Jennifer was waiting for me. I handed over the large coat box with trembling hands and misty eyes. "Thanks, Mom, for doing this. Emily was so afraid she wouldn't get to wear her coat. Mom, what's wrong? Why the tears?"

"Jen, you probably don't remember my telling you, but when I was seven I wore the coat for Christmas, too. I felt like a princess. That is why I really wanted Emily to have it. My mom will be so pleased to see another one of 'her girls' wearing it again."

"Oh, wow, Mom! I forgot that you wore the coat, too. We've started a tradition, kinda like the passing of the Olympic torch," she said as her eyes glistened. "I just wish your mom could see Emily performing in that coat tonight."

"I'm sure she will, Jen. Heaven has the best seat in the house."

Sallie A. Rodman

A Mother's Hand

I stared in confusion,
at my left hand,
looking at the wrinkles,
around my wedding band.

It was a hand,
that was very well known,
but the hand that I saw,
wasn't my own.

The hand belonged to someone,
I'd loved as a child,
my maternal grandmother,
who was gentle and mild.

This hand had soothed,
and comforted me at night,
as it chased away,
my childhood fright.

Firm when it paddled,
my little behind,
when I was defiant,
refusing to mind.

As I stared it became,
the hand of another,
it was the loving hand,
of my dear mother.

This hand had guided me,
all through my life,
as a child, a teen,
and then as a wife.

It had patted and bandaged,
chased pain away,
been ready to help anytime,
night or day.

Suddenly the hand,
is once again my own,
as I realize a mother's hand,
is only a loan.

Passing from mother to daughter,
like the color of eyes or hair,
to insure future generations,
of kind loving care.

Pamela Gayle Smith

How?

It is better to know some of the questions than all of the answers.

James Thurber

We stood together at the funeral parlor, mother and son. I squeezed his hand hard to let him know I loved him as we said good-bye to his daddy.

Travis was ten years old. *How would he understand? How would he get through?* I worried to myself.

I slipped a locket into the casket. It held a picture of Travis and me. Travis placed a Hot Wheels car on the satin. Two gifts. Two good-byes.

He grieved quietly, to himself, sobbing only when we were in the privacy of our home, when he was behind his closed bedroom door, far away from my touch and concern, deep under the comfort of his blanket that muffled the sound of his voice.

"It's going to be okay, honey. You'll see." Mother words. Comforting words. What did they mean? They sounded plastic and empty, even to my own ears. *How could I replace a man? How could I replace a father? How could I fill that hole?*

Travis's daddy was his hero. No one was as strong. No one was as fast. No one was as funny.

His teachers used to say, "Travis is so full of life." And he was. But now? Helplessly I watched grief chip away pieces of his heart. He didn't laugh like he did before. His eyes lost their mischievous sparkle.

"Everybody else has their daddy," he told me. "Why can't I have mine?" How do I answer that?

He quit karate classes: "It's no fun without Daddy watching me."

He quit Little League: "It's no fun if my daddy can't watch me play."

Honey, if I could bring him back, I would. If I could put salve on your scratched heart, I would. But I'm not God; I'm just a mother. I don't understand why it happened, either. I have questions, too, like, "How do I teach you about girls? How do I teach you to be strong? How do I teach you to be a man?" Time doesn't heal wounds completely, but it does make the scars a little lighter.

Little by little he rebounded. Day by day, part of the natural process, his infectious laugh returned, his sense of humor, the life in his eyes. Once again we were wrestling on the living room floor and playing baseball outside in the yard.

My boy was back, but my questions still remained. *Who would be his role model? His hero?* He had uncles and grandfathers, but they weren't in his life every day. He needed something more. Someone who cared deeply about what happened to him and who would move heaven and earth to help him be the best he could be.

"Please, Lord," I prayed, "show me how to be the kind of parent he needs."

I wasn't sure if I could be any kind of parent then, wondering if my half-hearted attempts were enough. His dad was my childhood sweetheart, and I was dealing with heartache of my own. I read books on grief and bereavement for my son and myself, and it all made sense on the surface, but not underneath. I was a social worker, supposed to know the answers or be able to find them, and normally I did, but now I was the one who needed a social worker, someone who could say the right thing, tell me where to go, how to manage the turmoil of emotions. My emotions for my son were tidal waves crashing in, and all I could do at the time was give it all to the Lord.

About a year after my prayer, I sat on the porch swing, and he came to sit down with me, carrying a book of beautiful muscle cars—Mustangs, Novas, GTOs, Chargers, Dusters.

"Remember when you got me this book last year, Mom?"

"Sure do."

"And, remember when you took me to see that classic car show?"

"I sure do."

"And the time you took me fishing?"

"Yes, I remember."

"And bowling? And skating? And swimming? And the time we built an igloo?"

"Sure. I remember all of that."

He smiled at me and handed me a folded piece of paper. "Open it up and read it."

I did, and it was a paper he had written for school. A big red A was at the top of the page.

The title of the paper was, "My Hero," and the words read: *My hero is my mom. I want to be just like her when I grow up. She teaches me right from wrong, and she wants me to be a good man.*

Hot tears filled my eyes, and we hugged.

"Thank you, Travis," I whispered. "I love you."

Tammy Ruggles

3

LEARNING AND TEACHING

Nothing in life is to be feared, it is only to be understood.

Marie Curie

As the Snow Flies

If we don't change, we don't grow. If we don't grow, then we aren't really living.

Gail Sheehy

As the season's first snow fell, I realized that my two-year-old daughter probably had no recollection of this fascinating occurrence from the first two winters of her life. With wide eyes, she looked out her bedroom window, delighted and intrigued, wanting to know where the snow was coming from, not able to stay still or listen long enough to hear the answer.

As is usual during the afternoons when just the two of us are home, I feel compelled to rush her to bed for her nap. Our lives have become so busy, and straying from our routine seems to send the rest of the day into upheaval. Without a lengthy nap, Elena has a difficult time making it through the day, and I had work deadlines to meet as well as the usual household chores. *Tomorrow*, I thought often, *we'll slow down*. But along with each tomorrow comes a new set of tasks and priorities that can't wait.

But today, I wanted to not care at all. The snow was falling, and as far as Elena could tell, it was an entirely new experience. She was fascinated by the large, fluffy flakes, and watched intently as each one fell diagonally and with great speed, settling on the trees, the rooftops, and the ground below.

We went into the living room and aimed a rocking chair toward the large glass door that overlooked the backyard. I found the melodic lullaby CD I used to play when she fell asleep for her nap. So many memories came flooding back as I remembered the music that was as much a part of our routine as feeding time. I remembered the baby she used to be.

We rocked in the chair, her head resting on my chest, as we watched the snow fall. I desperately hoped that I could remember this moment forever, or at least long enough to remember the importance of slowing down from time to time. I know children are adaptable, but I wondered why we need them to be so. Often when I play with my kids, I am struck by how simple it is to amuse them, how anything can be turned into an exciting game. A child's first experience watching the snow fall should not be rushed, but savored and appreciated for the wonder and absolute joy it elicits.

As I held my daughter, who had nearly tripled in size since our earliest days together, I thought about the many changes that had transformed her from a tiny baby into such a delightful little girl, all of the changes that, incredibly, had happened right before my eyes. As I was reminiscing, "Twinkle, Twinkle, Little Star" began to play, and I remembered that, as a baby, she would usually be asleep by now. But instead, she lifted her head and insisted we sing together. I did, but stopped because I wanted to hear only her. I wanted to enjoy the adorable mispronunciations of a small child learning to speak, and relished how happily unaware she was that her words sounded different from mine.

I wondered how much of this music, if any, she recalled, and I smiled as I realized that, just as infants are soothed by the sounds heard while in the womb, I am comforted by the familiarity of this music that has transported me back to a time that now seemed a world away. A time before I had spent too many of our tomorrows on what might not have been a priority, after all.

That afternoon, a wonder of nature taught me a very important lesson about appreciating the simple things, because even though each and every winter has a first snow fall, there will never be another "first" snow fall for my little girl. And I will never forget, or regret, sharing it with her.

Paula McKee

Super Mom

My mom has superpowers . . .

My mom has the power to talk to the animals. She'd tell
me:
"My little birdie told me that you were speeding."
"My birdie said you were acting up in school."
That dumb bird always got me in trouble!

My mom has the power of invisibility. She would say:
"Behave yourself, always act like you would if I were in the
room."
"You never know when I might be watching."

My mom has the power of supersonic hearing. She would
tell me:
" I heard that!"
"Don't you dare talk to your sister like that."
How did she hear that? She wasn't even in the room—and
I didn't see that dumb bird of hers anywhere in sight.

My mom has the power of eyes in the back of her head.
  Her famous lines:
"Don't even think about it."
"I see you."
Only eyes in the back of her head could explain how she
  knew that it was me who broke her lamp.

My mom has the power to read minds. She would say:
"It looks like you had a bad day, want to talk about it?"
"I think you need some ice cream, let's just you and me go
  get some."

My mom has the power of having extra arms.
  She can help glue my science fair project, make my
  sister cookies for her class, and iron my dad's shirt.
  She has sewn a formal, cheered at a baseball game, and
  had dinner on by 6 o'clock. And she can do this *all at
  the same time.*

My mom has the power to heal:
She's mended many a broken heart with chocolate,
She put "pink stuff" on my chicken pox, on my poison ivy,
  and on my poison oak.
She held me when I cried all day because my cat died.
She gave me Band-Aids so I could heal my baby dolls.
I know that her kisses can make all things well.

My mom has the power to transform into a youth again:
She can hula-hoop better than anyone I know,
She can hokey pokey on roller skates,
And she still beats us all as we race across the pool.

My mom has the power of forgiveness:
She forgave me when I let the turtle climb her fancy new
  curtains.

She forgave me when I used her new perfume on all my
    baby dolls and stuffed animals.
She forgave me when I broke her blown glass figurine
    playing pillow football in the house.

My mom has superpowers.
    She is an extraordinary woman with extraordinary love.
    She has shared that love with me so that I, too, can be
    extraordinary.

The good news is now I'm a mom.
    And wouldn't you know it . . . I can feel them sprout-
    ing, even as we speak . . . eyes on the back of my head.
    Now, I just need to find me one of those birds!

Lynn Meade

Daughters Know Best

We were standing in a dressing room staring at the mirror. The object under scrutiny was a pair of jeans.

"Bend!" the younger woman in the tight little cubicle—my daughter—commanded, which I did. "Turn!" she said, and I listened.

I am no jeans expert, but this daughter clearly is. She knows her brands, her cuts, the minimum essentials of fit. She leads. I humbly follow.

If somebody asked me to pinpoint the precise moment when I began learning about jeans—and life—from my daughters, I probably couldn't do it. But something quite unsettling had been going on in my life. I found myself turning to my three daughters for a road map to everything, from where to go on the Internet to find an obscure line of eighteenth-century British poetry, to how to introduce shitake mushrooms into a salad.

I used to attempt casualness when I found myself floundering, a bit reluctant to acknowledge that, more often now, I feel a bit lost in the world that seems to belong to their generation. I used to pretend I was just grazing around in Jill, Amy, and Nancy's collective wisdom, because accepting this reversal felt humbling, even embarrassing.

Once, I was the queen of wisdom. I doled out advice, and they took it, at least until three fierce adolescences set in. But even then, I took on the role of a consultant on the thorny issues.

The decades slipped away. My daughters left me for campuses where I could occasionally glimpse their lives, but never fully know them. They fell in love; they traveled; they married; they had babies and careers.

My years of sweeping change seemed to end as theirs began. And they are smart! The older I got, the more amazed I was about how much they knew. When I felt particularly stupid or naïve, I had to remind myself that these daughters of mine were the beneficiaries of the powerful women's movement that came along just a tad too late for me.

Jill, Amy, and Nancy didn't have to deal with a world owned and run entirely by men. They were not constantly nervous, apologetic, or uncertain . . . traits I know all too well. And they deftly avoided bowing to the twin gods of caution and conformity—old pals of mine.

I was a senior in college when I met and married the second man who asked me. The first danced well, but had no character, which I somehow sensed even at age twenty. The one I married had lots of it, and was an older man of twenty-seven. I went from college to marriage with no stops along the way.

Miraculously, wonderfully, we're still together. And in those intervening years, I've finally grown from girl to woman to person. But there were still so many gaps. Not for our daughters, though, who shared dormitory floors with men in universities that had never deigned to open their wrought iron, ivy-covered gates to my generation of women. My daughters' generation of women married later, with more focus, and with strong identities all their own.

So increasingly, I would find myself borrowing from Jill, Amy, and Nancy's enormous stash of self-confidence and certainty. They had it to spare.

I'm playing catch-up. They're not.

More recently, I've just come right out and asked for help. It's easier and more honest than the pretense of nonchalance. I can't tell whether it makes me seem appealingly vulnerable to my daughters, or just someone in need of tolerant sympathy.

But oh, what I've learned. My daughters have taught me, without ever preaching, that life is an adventure, that even a woman who never played a single sport seriously, because only boys did that, still can learn the exhilaration of a fit body. They have demonstrated that it is possible to fit three weeks' worth of clothes into one small suitcase.

They've convinced me to experience yoga, subscribe to at least one politically correct magazine, and test myself with a vegetarian diet. I flunked.

My daughters have convinced me that women friends are to be cherished because, most of the time, they give unconditional love and support. And when I feel like an imposter as a writer, wife, mother, and human being, my women friends will convince me that I'm not. Or at least make me laugh at myself.

From these three strong, sure young women, I've learned to occasionally brush off my misgivings and wear something slightly outrageous, often from a thrift shop. My addiction to these places is a direct result of their initiation.

Most of all, I have been reminded by my daughters that these are not the Doris Day/white picket fence 1950s, even as I struggle with my own ghosts of those years. In the tangle of colliding images and possibilities, it's still sometimes hard to get my footing in the ongoing process of giving birth to myself.

Sally Friedman

A Cup of English Tea

Gratitude is not only the greatest of virtues, but the parent of all the others.

Sir Winston Churchill

"Oh, for the words I might have said, the things I might have done." My eyes were riveted to the inscription beneath the oil painting. Unlike the light and airy Impressionist paintings my mom and I had seen that day at the Art Institute of Chicago, this masterpiece depicted a somber funeral wreath on a glossy black door. The Monets receded from my memory, but this poignant inscription seared its way into my consciousness: "Oh, for the words I might have said, the things I might have done." What finality!

On the subway ride home, I thought about Mom. She sat close beside me, yet she was so distant. There were many things I could have said to Mom or done for her, but I didn't. *Now that I'm in college, I wonder if it's too late*, I thought.

Storybook vignettes of the past flashed before my mind. As a young daddy's girl, every night after dinner I sat on his lap and proudly slipped the paper ring from his Roy Tan cigar onto my finger. Instead of helping Mom with the dishes, Dad and I worked a picture puzzle. When my girlfriend slept over, Dad played a prank by putting Jell-O in the foot of my bed. After he got the surprised reaction he wanted from me, he tried to clean up the strawberry delight with a towel. But it was my servant mom who wiped my toes, changed the linens, and laid out fresh towels. Funny, I don't recall thanking her for her services.

As I grew older, Dad and I, each with a long stride, walked quickly down the street, while Mom, with her shorter legs, lagged farther and farther behind. Occasionally we paused to wait for her, but never long enough for her to catch up.

At a recent big gathering, I tucked my arm in Dad's and stayed close by his side, while Mom was the furthest thing from my mind.

The subway jolted to a stop. *From now on, it's going to be different. I want Mom to see how much she means to me.* I stole a glance at her seated beside me, prim in her suit and hat, her mind somewhere else.

"What are you thinking, Mom?"

"Oh, just about the troubled girls at my school."

Mom was a devoted teacher, and I knew she helped disadvantaged children in a number of ways. But I hadn't realized before now how deeply she felt for these children. *I wonder if I really know her. I guess I only know about her.*

That night, I gave Mom the hug usually reserved for Dad. She stood somewhat awkwardly, almost like a child who didn't know how to respond.

Lying in bed I asked God, *Please show me what I can do to reach her with my love.* Then it occurred to me that perhaps her British heritage was the key. *After all, she likes everything English. Maybe I can even try to change my tomboy persona, which often conflicts with her ladylike preferences.*

I asked the next day, "Mom, could we have a cup of English tea together this afternoon?"

Startled, she replied, "Why, yes . . . of course, dear."

I noticed how carefully she laid out her best china with silver teapot, pitcher of cream, and bowl of sugar, even adding a plate of Scottish shortbread, my favorite. She set the tea service on the low table and poured the tea she had brought back from England. As we held our cups and saucers somewhat stiffly, we talked about her recent trip to Cornwall to search out her relatives.

From that day forward, our tea party was repeated, each afternoon at three, just like clockwork. Soon formal talk became relaxed chatter. She gave our chat time a name, "girlie gab," and giggled like a schoolgirl when Dad came around to see what we were up to. She even unlocked the longings and secrets of her heart. Each day our lives were woven together more tightly.

Throughout the summer, we took an oil painting class, planted geraniums in big pots, shared our favorite historic novels, and excitedly discussed the book she was writing. But no matter how full our days, every afternoon we took time out for our cup of English tea.

In later years, and for too many of them, my marriage took me miles away from her—that is, until the autumn of her life. Dad had passed on, she suffered a mild stroke, and I longed once again to intertwine our hearts like the branches of a vine. So I brought her back East with me. This was the summer to delight her with the laughter of children and the playfulness of puppies. It became the autumn to shuffle through leaves, feed the ducks, and picnic by the brook. It turned into the winter to snuggle by the fire, carol at the piano, and peruse family photos. It broke into the spring to sniff country lilacs, hear the mockingbird's song, and most important, to sip a cup of English tea—together.

Then it was over. My brother wanted her with him, and I agreed it was fair. I steeled myself for the looming finality of her departure for the Midwest. The book of the things I might have said and the things I might have done was closing. There was nothing more I could do.

"Good-bye, precious Mom," I said at the airport, through tears. Her soft and radiant smile of thanks was all I needed.

Another summer came and went before I laid a wreath at her gravesite, a personal wreath interlaced with bright memories. How transformed it was from the cold wreath in the Art Institute painting because I'd heard the plea of the artist to love before the hour had passed.

Margaret Lang

Angel Fern

The true meaning of life is to plant trees, under whose shade you do not expect to sit.

Nelson Henderson

It was that time again, Mother's Day, a magical day of surprises, loving tributes, and emotional hazards.

In the past, we had traveled all over the state, sitting three hours in traffic to meet "halfway," accommodating age, health, no transportation, exams, soccer games, infants, and infantile adults. This year I decided to stay home and invite everyone for a cookout. Hubby offered to do the cooking, and I would prepare a few things.

There would be fourteen of us: one vegetarian, one on the Atkins diet, another on the South Beach diet, and one who ate nothing but cheeseburgers. Also to be considered were two attendees who had high cholesterol, two with high blood pressure, one with gout, one who was lactose intolerant, and one who had a seafood allergy. But I knew from years of experience that once our guests hit that food table, diet amnesia would set in, and everything would disappear in record time. So I prepared a black bean salsa with nachos, a crabmeat dip with seaweed crackers, a cheese/pepperoni/red grape platter, hot stuffed mushroom canapés, a sushi platter, assorted nuts, extra lean burgers, a dozen natural casing hot dogs, soy burgers and bratwurst, six pounds of extra large shrimp, two pounds of homemade coleslaw, three pounds of homemade potato salad, a crock of homemade baked beans, a large salad, strawberry shortcake with buttery biscuits and real whipped cream for dessert, and plenty of soft drinks, iced tea, and coffee, regular and decaf. I was ready for Mother's Day!

Needless to say, by then I was in a cranky mood as I set the table with cute little fishy plates and cute little fishy cups and cute little fishy napkins representing my Cape Cod lifestyle. *Mothers are supposed to have the day off. Be pampered. Be appreciated,* I muttered to myself.

Full into my "this-is-the-last-time" rant, I thought I heard a knock on the front door. It was so soft that I could barely hear it. Looking out of the kitchen window, I couldn't see any car, but decided to check the front door anyway. A tiny woman about eighty years old, beautifully dressed, stood on the front step. "This used to be my house," she said softly, and although we had never met the previous owner, I did recognize her name. I asked her if she would like to come in, and she was delighted.

I told her how much we loved the house, and as we walked from room to room together, she shared my excitement as I pointed out some of our recent updating projects. We had bought the house furnished, and when we came to her antique coffee table, her beautiful tall bookcases, and the many charming bedroom dressers that I had kept, she looked at me fondly and began to reminisce.

It had been their summerhouse for many years, her husband and six children. She remembered them all sitting on the living room floor around that coffee table eating their evening suppers. She recalled lovingly polishing each antique piece. And at the tiny bathroom, she laughingly recalled sharing it with her five daughters, "like a dormitory."

When we came to the kitchen and she saw her big antique table set and waiting, there was a longing in her voice as she asked about my family. She declined my offer to join us, and after thanking me with a big hug, she left.

A half-hour later there was that same soft knock at my door. There she stood holding a lovely plant, an Angel Fern. She thanked me again and again for my kindness, and said I had made her day. We hugged and wished each other a Happy Mother's Day, and then she was gone.

I stood and looked at my lovely Angel Fern, and then at my table set for family, and I was overwhelmed with gratitude.

Avis Drucker

More than Just a Pie

To praise is an investment in happiness.

George M. Adams

I was making a pie this afternoon and thought of my mother. It wasn't her pastry expertise that brought her to my mind as I carefully rolled the dough with the rolling pin I inherited from her kitchen, but the lack of it. I feel very accomplished every time I made a pie; I would gingerly lift it out of the oven and present it to my family like a work of art. My husband looks at me with an expression that says, "It's beautiful, but sheesh, it's just a pie!" If he only knew.

I am the product of eccentric lineage. My mother, although loving, could more appropriately be described as bizarre. While the mothers of my childhood friends baked cookies and hosted bridge parties, mine dabbled in the cross-pollination of strawberry plants and the breeding of tropical fish. While other mothers arranged flowers and reupholstered furniture, mine candled chicken eggs and nursed wild creatures back to health. She blatantly did her own thing. When I reached my teens and it was time to rebel, I became conservative.

Cooking was never my mother's strong suit; although she always put a meal on the table, it generally lacked enthusiasm. We were a basic meat-and-potato family. She was, however, adventurous when it came to trying new products—I was probably one of the first children on our street to taste instant potatoes.

Baking at our house consisted of a family pack of Dad's cookies. Once in a while, she would try her hand at a cake mix, or on a couple of occasions, a pie. Premade pie shells were yet to be invented; my mother's pastry was produced from instant sticks—the type she would crumble into a bowl, add a tablespoon of water to, and mix vigorously with a fork. The mixture would be dumped onto a floured countertop where she would attempt to roll it into the shape of a pie. The process never worked—her piecrust always looked like a 500-piece puzzle painstakingly pushed together. We were too young to care.

Her lack of domesticity was overridden by a flamboyant interest in all things living—animals, plants, and an ever increasing assortment of kids. My friends thought she was totally cool. She let us play our music in the living room, and she always had enough pork chops to be able to squeeze another place at the table for whoever wanted to stay for dinner. Mostly, she had time to talk—or more important, to listen.

Mom was gifted when it came to communicating with teenagers. She had a no-nonsense approach that bordered on tough, but it was served with such delicacy it was easy to swallow. Our home was always loaded with kids, many of whom dropped by just to talk to her.

As I rolled my pastry in long even strokes and watched the increasing smooth circle form, I thought about how my mother's pie shell mirrored her life—500 pieces pushed and molded together to form a unit into which she could pour a filling. Far from perfect, but strong enough to do the job.

Elva Stoelers

Oh, Christmas Trees

I can still recall the butterflies that took flight in my stomach when my mother told me that we would be purchasing not one, but two Christmas trees. To the ears of a little girl, more beautiful words had never been spoken.

I immediately assumed that the addition of a second Christmas tree would serve the sole purpose of creating additional space for gifts. Regrettably, this was not the case. One tree was for my mother to decorate by herself in elegant white lights and sparkling crystal angels, while the ornamentation of the second would be left to the discretion of my younger brother and me. Quite obviously, these two trees would be at opposite ends in the spectrum of aesthetic taste.

That first year of having two trees marked the beginning of a family tradition. Each December, my mother worked tirelessly perfecting her masterpiece, which in its completion, hovered ethereally in an outward-facing window for all to see. If prizes were awarded for beautiful Christmas trees, my mother would undoubtedly have taken home the blue ribbon. Its perfectly spaced spiral of twinkling white lights was echoed by a band of gold chiffon ribbon, which together set the stage for an array of luminous angels. The combined effect of its supernatural strength and extreme delicacy was enough to cause anyone to wonder if this tree grew from the soil of heaven itself.

However, if you were to turn and walk about twenty paces to the left, you would be confronted with a different Christmas tree. In place of the spiraling gold chiffon, strings of popcorn were strewn in a seemingly careless manner among colored lights, some blinking, others not, all equally irregular in their placement. In contrast to our mother, my brother and I had no theme for our tree, unless, of course, macaroni smothered in Elmer's glue and an abundance of Popsicle sticks could be considered a theme. Unlike our mother's tree, ours shared the joys of sticky hands and painstaking concentration. In short, it boasted of imperfection, an imperfection that was ours alone.

As a child, I always preferred our playful tree to our mother's elegant one. However, in my maturity, I have come to appreciate the value of each tree separately, or perhaps, the value generated by the presence of both together. The first declared the perfection we often expected from ourselves and others, while the second told the story of real-life experiences. I learned that we must keep our lofty ideals in one pocket and earthly practicalities in the other, because we, like Christmas in my household, would be otherwise incomplete. Who's to say that macaroni trees don't line the forests of heaven?

Ellen Brown

READER/CUSTOMER CARE SURVEY

We care about your opinions! Please take a moment to fill out our online Reader Survey at **http://survey.hcibooks.com**.

As a **"THANK YOU"** you will receive a **VALUABLE INSTANT COUPON** towards future book purchases

as well as a **SPECIAL GIFT** available only online! Or, you may mail this card back to us.

(PLEASE PRINT IN ALL CAPS)

First Name	MI.	Last Name

Address		City

State	Zip	Email

1. Gender
- ❑ Female   ❑ Male

2. Age
- ❑ 8 or younger
- ❑ 9-12   ❑ 13-16
- ❑ 17-20   ❑ 21-30
- ❑ 31+

3. Did you receive this book as a gift?
- ❑ Yes   ❑ No

4. Annual Household Income
- ❑ under $25,000
- ❑ $25,000 - $34,999
- ❑ $35,000 - $49,999
- ❑ $50,000 - $74,999
- ❑ over $75,000

5. What are the ages of the children living in your house?
- ❑ 0 - 14   ❑ 15+

6. Marital Status
- ❑ Single
- ❑ Married
- ❑ Divorced
- ❑ Widowed

7. How did you find out about the book?
(please choose one)
- ❑ Recommendation
- ❑ Store Display
- ❑ Online
- ❑ Catalog/Mailing
- ❑ Interview/Review

8. Where do you usually buy books?
(please choose one)
- ❑ Bookstore
- ❑ Online
- ❑ Book Club/Mail Order
- ❑ Price Club (Sam's Club, Costco's, etc.)
- ❑ Retail Store (Target, Wal-Mart, etc.)

9. What subject do you enjoy reading about the most?
(please choose one)
- ❑ Parenting/Family
- ❑ Relationships
- ❑ Recovery/Addictions
- ❑ Health/Nutrition
- ❑ Christianity
- ❑ Spirituality/Inspiration
- ❑ Business Self-help
- ❑ Women's Issues
- ❑ Sports

10. What attracts you most to a book?
(please choose one)
- ❑ Title
- ❑ Cover Design
- ❑ Author
- ❑ Content

TAPE IN MIDDLE; DO NOT STAPLE

I₁ıIIııIIıIₐIₐIIₐIₐIₐIIIₐIₐIₐIₐIııₐIₐIₐIₐIₐI

FOLD HERE

Comments

Do you have your own Chicken Soup story
that you would like to send us?
Please submit at: **www.chickensoup.com**

The Best Role of All

What lies behind us and what lies before us are tiny matters compared to what lies within us.

Ralph Waldo Emerson

The bell rang, and I was free. I grabbed my sweater from the cloakroom, shouldered my red plaid book satchel, and followed the line out the door to the waiting yellow school bus. The day was over, and the other kids were laughing, but I was carrying a burden heavier than a book bag. All the way home I sat in silence, tears brimming. At the door of my house, the dam broke.

Thankfully, in this midfifties household, my mom was there to gather me in reassuring arms and gently probe to find the splinter in my soul. She consoled while I cried until at last I was ready to talk.

"Each class is giving a play at school," I sniffled, "and . . . and the first grade is doing Tom Thumb's wedding!"

"That's nice, honey. Do you have a part?"

"Yes . . . yes . . . I do." The heaving sobs returned.

"Are you nervous, dear?"

"No, Mom, I'm old." More tears!

"I have to be *old* . . . and I'm *only* six!"

At last, the soggy truth was told. All the parts had been given, and I got the role nobody wanted as the mother of the bride!

The only bride I knew was my mom. She had worn a pretty white dress in the picture on the wall in her bedroom. I knew and loved her mother—Mimi—my only grandmother, but I was not ready to be like her, at least not for a very long time. She made great cookies, but she was a little bit plump, wore glasses, and had gray hair! This was not the part I had imagined for my dramatic debut.

Mom's reassuring smile melted my heart, and her gentle response could have won an Oscar. "Marcia, honey, you don't understand. You have been given the most important part!"

"What do you mean, Mom?" I was astonished.

"You and your friends don't realize it, but the mother of the bride has the honor of being the last person seated before the ceremony begins. She is so important that after she is seated, no guests are allowed to enter the sanctuary . . . the doors are closed. If anyone is late, they have to stay outside."

My mouth dropped open in awe of my new role.

"Come with me," she beckoned, and I mutely followed.

We walked into her bedroom and over to the dresser where she invited me to share the bench. This was a grown-up place, holy ground. As I marveled at the invitation, savoring the essence of face powder and Chanel No. 5, she opened her jewelry box, pulled out a tray, and retrieved the most brilliantly sparkling diamond bracelet I had ever seen. I could hardly breathe as she began to fasten it around my small wrist.

"You'll have to be careful," she cautioned, "because this bracelet is far too big for you and it will easily fall off your arm. But I'm going to let you borrow it for the performance. Mimi wore it when I got married. It is a mother-of-the-bride bracelet."

"Oh, Mom! This is so beautiful. And you would let me wear it?"

"You're the mother of the bride, aren't you? And mothers of the bride are very special."

"Are the diamonds real, Mom?"

"No honey, they are rhinestones, but it is expensive costume jewelry, so you must take very good care of it."

"Oh, I will, Mom!" I said, visibly relieved.

The night of the play, I faintly remember that I wore a long dress, and I'm sure it was very pretty, probably blue, and probably made by Mimi. They did seat me last. But the thing I remember most was walking down that aisle staring at my bracelet, watching it sparkle, feeling the weight of its significance and the honor I had been given to wear it. I decided right then that the role no one wanted was the best role of all.

Fast-forward fifty years. After a six-month engagement, my only daughter married in June. Weeks of joyous preparation culminated in a midsummer night's dream. And for the second time in my life, I played the mother of the bride. This time there were only tears of joy. Hair color now hides the gray, Weight Watchers shaved the pounds, and contact lenses had long ago replaced spectacles. Once again my dress was long and pretty, rose instead of blue, but not made by Mimi. She and Mom were watching from heaven. I knew it the moment I snapped the clasp on my bracelet, as brilliant as ever. It finally fit, and so did the role. I still believe it is the best role of all.

Marcia M. Swearingen

The Last Sofa

It had to be white, or at the very least, off-white.

The sofa that my mother knew would be her last on this earth could not be dark or murky or even neutral. It would be a bold statement that at last, at very long last, she would own a wildly impractical sofa.

And why not?

Why should a woman in her nineties shop for a sofa that is durable or sensible? Why shouldn't she go for broke and find a sofa that's the polar opposite of every other sofa she's owned in her long and practical life?

So there we stood on a recent afternoon, mother and daughter, surveying a slick leather sofa in chocolate brown, a four-seater in maroon velvet, several handsome tweeds in charcoal grays and beiges, and one free-form sofa in fiery red. To all of them, Mom said a firm, almost angry "No!"

Her determination was enough to startle several young salespeople who figured they had an easy mark here: go for the sensible tweeds, the won't-show-a-thing darks with this elderly little lady and be done with it.

Hardly.

If I was fading fast in the third store, Mom was not. The thrill of the chase had inspired her, energized her, and given her a free pass away from her apartment in an anonymous high-rise that, on some long days, must have felt like a prison.

On this day, Mom was the captain, and I was merely her lieutenant.

This was not, mind you, an extravagant woman—anything but. Born to Eastern European immigrant parents who owned a fruit store and put in impossible hours selling Bartlett pears and four kinds of apples, Mom knew few indulgences. And while her lot in life improved when she married my late father, it was still not improved enough to allow for white sofas.

The Depression mentality that began their marriage in the early 1930s stretched into decades. Spending money never came easily, and often never came at all. Making do was the modus vivendi, especially for my mother.

But even a woman who watched her pennies was finally ready to replace the sofa that had ushered in a second marriage. Mom had stuck with it long after Irv's death nearly twenty years ago. The quilting had flattened, and lately, the stuffing had oozed out of the pillows lining the couch's back.

"I'm ready for a new sofa," my mother had announced unceremoniously one day, and I felt like cheering. Seemingly out of the blue, there was this sudden mission to find my mother's last sofa. And maybe her most important purchase ever.

In the fourth store, my mother, cane in hand, prowled the sales floor. Sofa shopping had become a blood sport. And then she spotted it. Sitting quite alone was the most sensuous, lush white silk sofa with just the faintest off-white stripe. It might well have worn a sign that read "Keep Off!" It was that wildly impractical.

Mom circled the sofa, stood behind it, stood in front of it, and then lowered herself into its cushions. No queen was ever more regal than my five-foot, ninety-five-pound mother on her silk throne. I watched, dumbfounded, as my mother, besotted with love for this object of her desire, seemed to shed years and woes and intimations of mortality as she settled into that sofa's plump cushions.

And what was most striking was this woman, who had demanded to know the price of everything with something approaching ferocity, didn't even bother to look at the price tag dangling from this sofa. It seemed a nonissue.

Despite the thousands of hours we two had shopped together as mother and daughter—despite the daily phone calls and endless conversations about every subject imaginable—I understood, in that store, that there was a still a secret place in my mother's soul. And that secret place needed and wanted this last tango with something sumptuous and opulent, something she'd never had as a bride or a young mother or an empty nester or a lonely old woman.

I could never shovel into mere words the look on Mom's face when she learned that this sofa—this ultimate sofa—was also a floor sample, and therefore a markdown.

My mother lived to enjoy that sofa only six months. But even as her health failed, that white silk sofa with deep cushions and a slightly curved back gave her something to relish every day.

"How I love that sofa!" Mom said to me on one of her last days on this earth.

And we both understood that at last—at long last—my dear mother had been knowingly, deliberately, self-indulgent.

It was the last time I saw her smile.

Sally Friedman

4

ON LOVE

Being deeply loved by someone gives you strength; loving someone deeply gives you courage.

Lao-tzu

A Half-Ounce of Love

All that I am, or hope to be, I owe to my angel mother.

Abraham Lincoln

My mother made solid contact with me in flimsy forms. Each one weighed less than half an ounce. They were air letters, sheets of blue paper prestamped, folded, and sealed to make narrow envelopes. My memories of them have lasted years after her death.

Air letters came from my mother each week with clock-like regularity. They came each week for a quarter of a century, the flimsy pale blue of them sheltered between sturdier pieces of mail. I welcomed my mother's handwriting. We were thousands of miles apart. When I first left England for my new home in the United States, I was desperately homesick. Along with air letters came parcels containing gravy browning mix, custard powder, my favorite tea, and sometimes chocolates. There was always the weekly letter, which was far more important than the food. I could not wait to reply. I was eager to respond to generate more mail.

Each Thursday, for a quarter of a century, I sat down by

the window with a blank air letter in front of me. I filled it easily, turned it overleaf, sealed it, and walked to the mailbox. I knew my mum would be doing the same thing.

What did we write about? What sustenance did my mother provide me? She told me Aunt Winnie had visited, Cecil's Labrador dog had chewed up a leather glove, the cactus had flowered, and she had new yellow curtains in the kitchen.

I replied that Tim had made the honor roll, the cat had jumped into the punch bowl at my party, and my tulips were blooming. Our handwriting softened sad news and illuminated joyful incidents. She had no telephone for many of those years; a telephone call usually meant bad news. The air letters that followed gave more details, expressed the thoughts behind the tragedies. When my brother Derek's son was killed in an accident, I was unable to leave St. Louis because of an ice storm. Mum described the gathering after the funeral. She wrote that Derek made endless cups of tea for everyone. Her words said it all.

Each of her letters to me began, "We were so pleased to get your letter, dear." She was pleased. She welcomed my words. She wanted all the details of my family, dogs, plants, meals, and fortunes, good and bad.

When I replied, I wanted to be proud of what I had done that week. It was good to say that I had attended church, cared, and shared my skills and talents. Many an action of mine was curtailed when I began to wonder how I would write about it to my mother. The words on the air letters, carefully folded and sealed, were the story of my life unfolding in a strange country.

She wrote until three weeks before she died.

Mum's sustenance and caring led our whole family to a routine of keeping in touch with each other. Some of us now use e-mail, inexpensive telephone rates, and bargain flights across the ocean to stay in touch. Yet, when I think of my mother's letters, written in a quiet spot, folded, mailed, and received with such delight, I put pen to paper. There is no delete button for a written letter, no backspace to eat up whole sentences. Each word is carefully measured before being mailed.

My family and I honor the memory of my mother's never failing half-ounces of love. Mischievous dogs, new curtains, blooming plants, and luscious meals are still described. Mum provided us with the groundwork, bless her dear heart.

Sylvia Duncan

The Heartbeat

Lying in wait,
Anxious eyes on the screen.
Colors of gray and white,
But what do they mean?

The nurse finds a spot,
She says, "Look here."
I strain as she continues,
"That is a baby, my dear."

My eyes well with tears,
My breath hangs in my chest.
Such a beautiful image,
By far the best.

Just a spot on the screen,
Not a distinguishable part.
Till she shows me some more,
The beat of a heart.

So small and yet fast,
The beat is so strong.
Proving there is life,
Proving nothing is wrong.

My own heart is beating,
I fear it may break.
The amount of love that I'm
feeling,
It surely can't take.

I stare at your picture,
My eyes finally dry,
Then I smile and I whisper,
"See you in July."

Susan J. Krom

Not Just on Mother's Day

*Keep your face to the sunshine and you cannot
see the shadow.*

Helen Keller

I do not need gifts on Mother's Day. I have the gift I
want and need. It is the gift of motherhood. It cannot be
purchased in department stores or stacked on shelves. It
cannot be created in a factory. It cannot be wrapped in a
box. Nor can it be limited to one day. Motherhood is every
day. And every mother knows it.

I lost my mother when I was twenty-six years old. I
had thought we would be together for many years. I had
not even considered life without her. We were friends,
best friends. Her first grandchild had just been born, and
life's possibilities had barely opened for me when she
passed on. It took many years for me to recover. Twenty-
six years seemed such a short time to have my mother.
To have her love. Her protection. Her devotion. To enjoy
her beauty and zest for life. She would not see me
become a mother again, or any of the things I would
accomplish later in life. We were just beginning to know

each other as adults. I ache to call just one more time, "Mother," and have her answer. And see her face. And tell her the things I might have been too busy to say. Oh, how I long to say them now. Not just on Mother's Day. But every day.

I see the family photographs of my mother holding me. Holding my brother. I wanted to ask her so many things as a young mother. Was she as frightened as I was that I would not be suitable for the job? Did she doubt everything about herself and wish there had been some course she could have taken that would have prepared her for this new life she held in her arms? What did she wish she had taught me? What did she want me to teach my children? And even now, had she lived, I would have liked to care for her in older age as my children care for me. Not just on Mother's Day. But every day.

Before becoming a mother, I only knew about having a mother. I only knew what I needed of her. She taught me to walk with my back straight, my head up. She taught me to believe in myself. She protected me whenever I needed it, and let me go when I needed that, also. But I did not know about being a mother until I had children. The world of motherhood tested me. It asked me to be better than I thought I might be. Stronger. Wiser. Braver. And it never took a day off. Whether sick or tired or frustrated or defeated, mothering continued. Not just on Mother's Day. But every day.

The world of motherhood is generous. It embraces anyone who has the gift of mothering. It welcomes everyone who might bring comfort to humanity. It is not just for those of us who see our own faces in our children's, but also for those who offer a mother's touch when needed.

Forty-six years later, I wear the title of "Mother" proudly. It demands even more of me now: to set an example, make my children proud, give them strength and support, be there when needed, and to always be their biggest fan.

Not just on Mother's Day. But every day.

Harriet May Savitz

The Beauty of Alzheimer's

To keep the heart unwrinkled, to be hopeful, kindly, cheerful, reverent—that is to triumph over old age.

Thomas Bailey Aldrich

My mother is losing her eyesight, so when we get together, I read the clues to her, so she can still do crossword puzzles.

"It's a long word," I say. "It means 'tardy one.'"

"Latecomer?" she responds. *Darn, how does she do that? I wonder to myself.* It's hard enough to do crosswords when you're looking at the squares and the adjoining letters, but somehow, she pulls the words right out of thin air.

"That's right! I can't believe you got that one. But this one's a little harder. It's kind of a long word. It means 'abodes' and starts with 'D.'"

"Dwellings?" she answers. *Amazing.* She's right again.

I scan the puzzle, trying to find one I would know the answer to. *Nope. Not that one. Not that one either.* There are some I know she won't get; she never associates "wooden golf ball holder" to a "tee." After all, she never played golf. But she knows that the high card in a deck is an "ace" and the dance that they do in Hawaii is the "hula."

Big deal, you may be thinking. Well, to me it is a big deal. My mother has Alzheimer's.

She doesn't have the almost fully functional Stage 1 of Alzheimer's that allows people to still live at home and sometimes hold down a job. She's way up to Stage 6 (out of seven stages) and has been in that stage for almost five years now. Sometimes she doesn't know my name. She doesn't know where she is (in a nursing home) or why she's there. But she's still really good at word association, which allows us to still do crossword puzzles. I'm sure she hasn't used any of these words in a sentence in a very long time. I mean, how often do you use words like "dwelling" or "latecomer" anyway? But she was always great with words, having spent her whole life doing crossword puzzles and playing Scrabble

Some people get really mean and nasty at this stage of Alzheimer's. I hear them at the nursing home, arguing and yelling at the other residents and at the nurses. My mother went the other way. She got nice, and she got happy. I mean *really* nice and happy, which was kind of unusual for her.

For as long as I can remember, my mother wasn't a happy person. She was negative and sarcastic and critical. I spent my whole life trying to please her and make her happy, and I never felt like I succeeded. I certainly never recall her telling me I was beautiful. Always somewhat depressed and shy and unassuming, now my mother starts singing and dancing whenever she hears music, regardless of whether she knows the words or the beat to the song.

She's also very talkative and is always bragging about me to everyone she meets.

For instance, as soon as I arrive for a visit, she says, "Let's go introduce you to some people." We walk the halls and she introduces me to the same people she has been introducing me to for the last two years. "This is my daughter," she says "Isn't she beautiful?"

The nicer nurses play along "Oh yes, Ruth. She's beautiful just like you." But some of the nurses are tired of playing the game. "I know it's your daughter," they say. "I've met her a thousand times." And some of the residents are way past the point of understanding what my mother is even saying. That doesn't faze Mom a bit. Two minutes later, when we run into the same person, she's at it again. "This is my daughter. Isn't she beautiful?"

We make our way down the hall, carrying out our meet-and-greet until Mom gets tired and wants to go back to her room. And since it's very hard to carry on a conversation with someone who can't remember what happened five minutes ago, we usually start in on our crossword puzzles. She lies down in bed and closes her eyes, and I read her the clues. It's remarkable the number of times she gets the answer right, even words that I haven't heard her speak in years.

It makes the whole thing not so bad. I mean, Alzheimer's is horrible, really horrible. But this is the first time in my mother's life that she seems really happy. It's certainly the first time I have ever seen her giddy enough to sing and dance. It's the first time that we've ever spent time together doing nothing but having fun and being supportive of each other.

And it's the first time in my life that I've learned that when she hears the word "daughter," she always associates it with the word "beautiful."

Betsy Franz

Sounds of Childhood

Peanut butter faces, handprints on the wall.
I see them running through the house, playing
   with a ball.
All the sounds of childhood,
fill my home with lovely noise.
But someday they'll grow up, move on,
and have their own little girls and boys.
So for now I will enjoy the ones that God has given
   me.
I will count my blessings every day.
For I am blessed indeed!

Jean Lockwood

The Mother of Boys

I am the mother of boys.

I play goalie as I make supper. I can dribble a ball as I answer the phone and can assemble a train as I nurse a baby.

I am the mother of boys.

I measure a good day not by the weather or the company, but by the number of bugs caught, the quality of the sticks found, and the depth of the puddles splashed.

I am the mother of boys.

Fascinated ears listen to me tell tales of alligators, dinosaurs, and fast cars. I do load upon load of blue laundry; the only pink item to be seen is when a red sock makes its way into the white load. I check all laundry for reptiles and rocks.

I am the mother of boys.

I most frequently say, "Not so rough," "Get down, please," and "Watch where you're peeing." I get dizzy watching little bodies run circles around any inanimate object.

I am the mother of boys.

I wipe forever-dirty faces and hands. At night, I am amazed by the many new bruises and scrapes. I join in prayers that thank God for airplanes and pirates and Smarties candies.

I am the luckiest mother on earth. I am the mother of boys.

Beverly A. Suntjens

Just Yesterday

A mother is not a person to lean on, but a person to make leaning unnecessary.

Dorothy Canfield Fisher

Just yesterday . . .

. . . I was a twenty-six-year-old mother bringing my first baby home from the hospital. An enchanted pastel-adorned and hope-filled nursery welcomed our young family of three.

. . . I nursed my infant son as I inhaled his sweet scent and nuzzled the silky fine wisps of newborn hair.

. . . I'd tiptoe into his room and listen to his quiet breathing and imagine the boy he'd one day become. Filling barely a corner of his crib, surrounded by soft, powder blue linens and indescribable love, he'd sleep.

. . . I addressed cards announcing the arrival of our miracle, declaring his father's and my unmitigated joy. I'd joke with my husband that this tiny baby would one day—in the faraway, faraway future—be part of the graduating class of 2003. How funny that sounded.

. . . middle-of-the-night feedings seemed endless and

exhausting, a car seat was permanently in the back of my car, a playpen was occupying space in the den, and a nightlight was lit in the upstairs hall.

. . . chocolate ice cream with rainbow sprinkles distracted tears and fears and cured just about everything that ailed my preschooler.

. . . my five-year-old son donned a backpack filled with crayons, glue, and a brand-new lunch box and posed wide-eyed with anticipation for the initial photo that would begin a tradition of capturing those first-day-of-school mornings forever.

. . . I cheered for him on the soccer field, kept close tabs on him in the pool, and waited outside a dressing room while he reluctantly tried on clothes.

. . . I'd remind him to say thank you and please, do his homework on time, keep up with his chores, and get ready for bed.

. . . the calendar flipped to a time when friends, girls, hair, and clothes took center stage in his life. And chaperoning field trips, holding his hand at the dentist, bringing birthday cupcakes to school, and meeting him at the bus stop halted abruptly in mine.

. . . he drove out of our driveway on his own and sampled the independence and freedom that loomed around just a few more childhood corners.

. . . conversations about college and plans for a time that no longer seemed so far off began to dominate all others.

. . . I purchased his last yearbook, wrote his last school note, and made his last sack lunch.

Today, that little boy's hairy legs dangle over the edge of his queen-sized bed, his whiskers tickle my face when he kisses me during a visit home, and a cell phone—not a baby monitor—alerts me with a deep, masculine voice that he's safe and sound. The days I thought might never end, the ones I wished wouldn't, the moments that I wore like a second skin, absorbed my every breath, infiltrated my every thought, were . . . just yesterday.

Lori Shaw-Cohen

Paradise

The shouts and screams of laughter
the toys spilled in the hall.
I pick up shoes and jackets
and put away a doll.

Cookie crumbs seem never-ending
clothes lie everywhere.
"Quiet" is a funny word;
In fact, it's rather rare.

Only when at night they sleep,
my children are calm and still.
Yet I yearn for noise and racket;
It makes my life fulfilled.

Others call it an annoyance.
"Absurd!" they say it is.
But I call my home "Paradise",
and I owe it all to kids.

Jennifer Lynn Clay

Three Little Girls

A mother is she who can take the place of all others but whose place no one else can take.

Cardinal Mermillod

I became a mom in 1965 when I married a man who had custody of his three little girls, ages seven, five, and three. People often ask me now, "How *did* you do that?"

I have to chuckle when they ask, because I really was too busy and too newly married to even think about how I did it—I just did it! I remember that it was not always easy, but I knew I was going to give it everything I had because I loved their father with all my heart. I turned twenty-one just two weeks after our wedding, and I was young and full of energy and optimism.

My stepdaughters desperately needed a stable family environment at that time, and they were open and receptive to my "mothering" and love. There were difficult situations to handle, because they were still getting used to a new person in the house. They were also dealing with the emotions that accompanied occasional visits with their mother. She would always be their mother and a part of their lives. I was amazed at the way they seemed to work it all out in their little minds and still be so accepting of me as their new caregiver. The phrase, "Love heals all things," comes to mind!

In a short time, I actually felt their love and acceptance, and it made the job of parenting much easier. But when I found that I was expecting my own child, I wondered just what my feelings might be after I gave birth. Would I feel the same about doing all the motherly things for them on a daily basis? Would I still enjoy my stepmother status, or perhaps resent the extra work that caring for the girls required?

Our son, Steven Vincent, was born on October 10, 1967. He was the first grandson in the family on my husband's side, and the grandparents were overjoyed. My husband finally had a son, and it was a happy occasion for all of us!

I remember being in the hospital after our son's birth, and recall the moment that I first gazed upon his little face lying next to me. The love that filled my heart was indescribable. I couldn't wait to hold him! I was a mother!

But my next thought was, "Wait! I am already a mother!"

Tears welled up in my eyes, as the volume of love seemed to increase inside my heart and soul. I missed those girls! I cried because I wanted to see them, to hug them, and have them meet their baby brother. It was the first thing I said to my husband when he came into my room.

"Can you bring the girls here?"

Back in 1967, they did not allow children in the maternity ward around the babies. I was pretty sure I would have to wait until my release from the hospital to see them. But my husband had an idea.

"I can bring them to the hospital, and you can look out the window. We will all be down there on the lawn."

Later that afternoon, I looked out of the hospital window and saw them with their Dad on the lawn. I remember it so clearly! Their blonde hair was shining, and their smiling faces looked up as they waved their little arms at me. It was such a pivotal moment in my life as I defined my family—our three girls and our new baby boy! The love I felt was again overwhelming, and I cried more tears of joy, surprising myself at the deep emotion I was feeling. My new son may have made me a biological mother, but I recognized the fact that I had already received the blessing of feeling motherly!

There were many challenges over the years as we added two more children to our family. I would not change one moment of any of it for the world! During some of the most challenging times with my stepdaughters, I would recall the day when I gazed down at them from that hospital window and realized just how very much I loved them.

Beverly F. Walker

Unconditional Love

Motherhood: All love begins and ends there.

Robert Browning

Thomas and I met my freshman year of college. We immediately found a comfort level with each other, despite our mutual inexperience with dating.

After the first year of dating, Mom asked me, "Do you see yourself marrying Thomas?" I said yes, I knew he was the one. Fast-forward a year and a half. I was lying in the backyard hammock at my parent's house, reading a book. It was the last bit of my life that would seem normal. I had a secret. I had kept it from my parents for five days because I was scared to death about the implications of this life-giving journey.

Mom joined me in the hammock on that June afternoon, an afternoon that changed everything. I put down my book and we swung next to each other. I just had to tell her. I didn't know how to begin, so I said, "Mom, will you always love me no matter what?"

She gripped me and said, "There is nothing you can do that will make me stop loving you."

"I'm in trouble."

"I know." She had found a small crumpled up sheet of paper in my trashcan as she emptied it the night before. On the paper were scribbled my thoughts, *Giving life versus doing what's easiest for me. Don't have all I want for a baby, but have lots of love to give.* My secret was out. The tears came bursting from my eyes, held in for too long. I knew my childhood was now behind me, and nothing would ever be the same. Worst of all was the fear that I had irreparably disappointed my parents.

The next weeks and months were a blur of family meetings, wedding planning, and doctor's appointments. It was the strangest blending of joy and sadness, bliss and anger that I ever felt. Mom and I had episodes of push and pull. It was a difficult realization that I would be leaving home a full year earlier than expected, my college graduation pushed back to accommodate the birth of my son. One particularly hard day left us both in tears and needing our distance. The next morning I found a rose in a dainty vase next to my bed with a note. It read:

To my dearest daughter: As beautiful as this rose is, you are more beautiful and precious to me. Never have you been a disappointment to me, only my source of greatest joy. Love, Mom.

Mom worked so hard to make my wedding day a joyful one, and it was. I wouldn't change anything about it. Thomas was welcomed into the family with a great celebration that spoke of grace. After the reception, I thanked my parents for a beautiful wedding and gave Mom a lingering hug. The guests blew bubbles as we sped off in the getaway car to our brief honeymoon. It wasn't until we got the pictures back from the photographer that I saw the tears in Mom's eyes as we left the reception.

Exactly six months after my wedding day, Mom was beside me and Thomas in the delivery room as we anticipated the arrival of the first grandchild. She was the one who placed him in my arms, my little Andrew William. She spent the first few nights with us and confidently comforted my screaming baby in the night, even though she was just as tired as I was. She came to my rescue on days I just couldn't get on top of the laundry or pull myself together to make dinner. She supported me emotionally, too, telling me often what a good mother I was.

On my first Mother's Day, she wrote me a letter:

To my dearest daughter, on this your first Mother's Day, I know full well that your road to motherhood has been an unexpected detour. Although you had not longed for a baby as I had, God still prepared your heart and will to be a wonderful mother to Andrew. Love him well . . . love him enough to give him your time, your joy, your discipline, your unconditional love. Mom

My mom and I have always had a special relationship. Even through the difficult teenage years we kept the lines of communication open. And when the hardest year in my life came, our friendship did not shatter. Instead, I learned of the deep, deep love a mother has for her child, a love that nothing can come between. I feel this love firsthand when I hold my son. I sometimes fear that I won't be able to protect him from the world. I fear that he will experience pain and sometimes have to learn lessons the hard way. But following Mom's example, I know I will love him unconditionally.

Rachel Lee Stuart

5

THROUGH THE EYES OF A CHILD

Who ran to help me when I fell,
  And would some pretty story tell,
  Or kiss the place to make it well?
  . . . my mother.

Jane Taylor

Jimmy's Question

Mother's love is peace. It need not be acquired, it need not be deserved.

Erich Fromm

It was obvious there was something on his mind as he watched me prepare dinner that evening. But with other people in and out of the kitchen, he did not say what he was thinking. I sensed he was waiting for everyone to be gone, so he could talk to me alone—to discuss something for our ears only, something important.

He was only eight years old when I met him. With his freckled face, blue eyes, and lock of blonde hair sweeping across his forehead, he looked as though he could have been Huck Finn, but of course he wasn't. His name was Jimmy.

For months he had mourned his mom's death, but now he really wanted to fill that void with a new mom. Just like his father, he was ready to "move on." When I married his father a short time earlier, I became Jimmy's mother—he became my son. But we all know a true mother-son relationship does not happen just because a legal document says we're related. It is always a decision made in the hearts of both parties involved.

Although the words were never spoken, right from the start Jimmy and I both knew what our relationship would be. I could tell from the way he treated me. He could tell from my response to him—and vice versa.

Soon thereafter came this evening in the kitchen when he asked the question that was on his heart, the question to which he needed to hear an answer in order to feel comfortable with this new person in his life. It did not matter that I was cooking dinner or that other people might come into the room. It could wait no longer. This was the moment he had chosen to ask me: "Is it okay if I call you 'Mom'?"

If ever there were a question that needed an immediate reply, if ever there were a response on the tip of one's tongue, this was it. I would not need time to consider my answer. After all, wasn't Jimmy the child whose head always rested on my shoulder when we were in church? Wasn't he the kid whose hand always found mine as we walked together? Didn't he resemble his father—the father with whom I had fallen in love? And wasn't this the little guy who had stolen my heart the first time I saw him?

And could there possibly be any doubt in my mind as to my response?

None whatsoever.

Joanne Wright Schulte

"I already have four girls. I picked out names for this one. If it's a girl, Jennifer, If it's a boy, hooray!"

Messy Kisses

When my grandson Beau was small, he would visit me on the weekend and delight me with his unusual antics. Being my first-born grandson, he could do nothing wrong, but at the same time, he was into everything. He especially loved to cook and would mix together peanut butter, chocolate, powdered sugar, and honey and would down the homemade concoction with orange and apple spice tea.

The first time Beau decided to eat his invention, I begged him to put it on bread. His response was that it tasted better without the bread because he could swish the "yuck" through his teeth, which he did with great gusto and lots of mess. Who was I to argue with the love of my life?

Seated at the table, drinking coffee and working a crossword puzzle, I heard someone behind me. Suddenly, Beau put his hands on my shoulders and planted a kiss on my cheek. The kiss, which included the peanut butter and other ingredients, slid down toward my chin, oozing and dripping with saliva. I was a mess!

Getting up from the chair, I walked over to get a paper towel to expunge the smell and clean my face. "GE, (hard g, long e, for "granny," because he couldn't pronounce the word) you just wiped off my kiss! Don't you like my kisses?"

Think fast, Joyce, I said to myself. "No, darlin', I love your kisses. I'm just giving myself a facial. Why, peanut butter and honey makes my skin feel like satin," I said as I wiped the paper towel all over my face.

Taking me by hand, Beau led me back to the table. "Let me see, GE." He lifted his sticky hands to my face and said, "You missed a spot. Here, let me rub it in." Before I knew what was happening, I was plastered with his peanut butter delight.

When he was young, Beau's facial became a part of our routine. It got to be that I loved the sticky mess, knowing his kisses could be so sweet. Many years later, when I think of him, I take out a jar of peanut butter, combine his tasty ingredients and slather it on my face. It may not be the best facial treatment on earth, but it sure brings back wonderful memories and his tender kisses.

Joyce Rapier

Blame It on Breastfeeding

Perception is merely reality filtered through the prism of your soul.

Christopher A. Ray

Breastfeeding had been making headlines again. Women around the nation had staged "nurse-in" events at local airports. They held the event to support a mother who was ordered off an airplane for nursing her daughter. I, too, am an ardent supporter of breastfeeding, having nursed all four of my sons. However, giving my children this healthy start has led to an unforeseen consequence—many years after weaning, they still consider me as the fount of all food.

My sixteen-year-old son wandered into the living room a few days ago. He plopped on the sofa and announced, "I'm hungry." I ignored him.

"Mom, I'm hungry. What can I have to eat?"

"The kitchen is less than six feet away, Ethan," I pointed out. "Go find something."

"But, I want you to tell me what to eat," he said plaintively. Plaintive, in a six-foot-tall teen who shaves, isn't appealing.

If it was just this son, I wouldn't feel so concerned. But his fourteen-year-old brother regularly comes home from basketball practice with this greeting, "What's for dinner?" That's it. No, "Hi, Mom." No, "How was your day, Mom?" Just, "What's for dinner?"

I can't blame this on my spouse. In twenty years of marriage, my husband has never greeted me with, "What's for dinner?" He knows his way around the kitchen and can feed himself.

On the drive home from school recently, I mentioned to the boys that their dad had a hard week at work. "Maybe I should work full-time, and let your dad be a stay-at-home dad for a while," I mused.

It was like all the air was sucked out of the car. "No!" gasped twelve-year-old Zack. "Bad idea, Mom," his four-teen-year-old brother concurred.

"Why?" I asked.

"We'd starve," said Alex

Zack agreed, " When I tell Dad I'm hungry, he says, 'Go fix yourself something to eat!'"

We spent the rest of the drive home in silence. The children, fearful their gravy train might leave the tracks, were subdued, while I absorbed the knowledge that I'm to blame for their lack of survival skills.

After talking with friends whose children feed themselves, I've started my New Year off with one goal—to have all four sons be self-feeders by spring. To that end, I've posted a list of available snacks on the refrigerator to circumvent the "what's to eat" question.

A few days into this new way of living, I was feeling much better. I'd kept guilt at bay, reassured by the fact that no one appeared malnourished.

I was working hard at my desk late one night when I felt a small presence beside me. I had a lot to do and very little time, so I just kept working. A sigh breezed past my ear. I looked up into the blue eyes of seven-year-old Sam. "Mom," he said, "I'm really hungry."

Knowing he'd walked past his father and past his three brothers to reach me, I took a deep breath. "Sam, there's a list on the refrigerator and other people who can help you."

"But, everything tastes better when you make it, Mom," he said.

I blame it all on breastfeeding.

Cindy Hval

"While Mom's away, Dad will be feeding us from the four major food groups: Canned, Frozen, Fast, and Junk."

Swing Time!

Our brightest blazes of gladness are commonly kindled by unexpected sparks.

Samuel Johnson

"Mom! Mom! Push us on the swing set!" my youngest daughter said, galloping out the front door, her pigtails bouncing like a pair of tossed Ping-Pong balls. That's my cue, I know, to put aside whatever I'm working on and follow her to our backyard. This is important—it was "swing time."

Fifteen years ago, after birthing my first child, I relied on our battery-operated infant swing to sooth my fussy six-month-old. The steady rhythm of the swing's motor never failed to drone my crying baby to sleep. Sometimes, I have to admit, I'd push my baby in the infant swing without even turning the power button on. I'd just push my sweet baby girl in her little swing by hand, completely absorbed in watching her fit her tiny fists in her drooling mouth or listening to the steady sucking sound she'd make in her sleep.

As each of my other five children grew up, they

introduced me to the wonderful world of outdoor play sets. My toddlers, preschoolers, even my school-age children never seemed to tire of swinging on their swing set. "Push me, Mommy!" they'd plead again and again. "Give me an underdog! Higher!" They'd giggle together, their long summer-blonde hair trailing behind them like wild angels' wings as they cut through the air, soaring higher and higher.

"I wish I had a battery-operated motor on our swing set," I confided in my husband at the end of one long summer day. "I feel like my arms will fall off after pushing so many kids on the swings all day. It'd be neat to just press a button, and all six swings would automatically push the kids as long as they want!"

My husband, ever the problem solver, jumped at the chance to use his ingenuity. "Well, I could rig up some kind of a motor to the framework . . . wonder how I could power the thing. Maybe I could . . ." But I had fallen fast asleep to the song of rusty swing hinges squeaking in my tired head.

Every day that summer and many summer days after, I'd push my children on our backyard swing set. Soon, my oldest daughters grew too tall to swing, their long legs dangling and dragging in the dust beneath the swing seat. But they'd still come out to the backyard with the littler kids and me to help push. They were better at giving "underdogs" anyway, they bragged. And I had to agree. While launching the little kids, my older girls tickled our toddler's toes, told knock-knock jokes with our kindergartener, and listened with bright eyes as their eight-year-old sister told them about the scary dream she'd had the night before.

Wow! This is great! I suddenly realized. For the first time in more than a decade, I didn't have to be the designated pusher. With my older kids to help, my younger children didn't need me to push anymore! Even the one-year-old was perfectly content to swing in his baby seat, buckled in safely, as my other children took turns pushing him and amusing him with their songs and games. *Who needed a battery-operated swing set now?* I thought. I could finally get a break from pushing now that my children could "pump" themselves and help each other. Sneaking from the lively swing set toward our house, I imagined the myriad ways I could spend my newfound time: I could catch up on the seven loads of laundry breeding in the hamper; I could read that novel I'd begun four times; I could go to the bathroom alone; I could . . .

Then I heard it. "Mom! Mom! Push us!" Looking back at the swing set loaded with my half-dozen children, I saw something I had never seen before. In the rhythm of their swings, that metronome-like to and fro, I saw the passing of time. I saw six beautiful children, completely capable of keeping each other swinging, completely content, and completely . . . grown. I understood then that in all those years of pushing my children on their swing set, the pushing was not the important thing. Granted, a battery-operated motor or a sister or their own two legs could keep them swinging. What was important to them was that I was there all those years, listening to their songs, hearing their happy voices, laughing at their jokes, and gazing in their bright eyes as we enjoyed our time on the swing set together.

I discovered that the swinging was not the thing. It was about love. About being a mom. About standing beside them, each of them, even when they were independent enough to do something without me. It was about being there simply to love them as they did what they loved to do. My children still wanted me there: to listen, to smile, to encourage.

But no longer did they need a mom to push them. Then

it hit me. Soon my children would need me to do something much more difficult than push: they would need me to let them go and watch them soar.

Cristy Trandahl

Pride and Prejudice

I found my mother sitting on the deck at the trailer, head exposed to the sun and ocean breezes. My trailer sits on a narrow part of a North Carolina sea island, and from the top deck, she could see both the turmoil of the ocean on one side of the island and the calm of the inlet on the other side.

But she was looking at neither. She sat staring into the lone, scraggly, wind-blown tree in the yard. A week after her first chemotherapy treatment, my mother's hair was already jumping ship, like her white blood cells and appetite. Big clumps of her hair had fallen out. The top was still full, but the sides showed missing patches. It was uneven and odd looking, like she had decided to become a punk rocker.

"Well, you didn't lose all of it," I said with a hug, after she noticed me looking at her head.

Mom seemed calm and steady. "I just want it all gone. It's going anyway. I'd rather not have it fall out in dribs and drabs. Let's get it all."

So we went in search of a hair salon with some available shears. The first place we stopped, a trendy little shop in a stucco-style strip mall, was full of young women. The hairdresser tossed her dark hair at us in welcome as we walked in, but when she got a closer look at Mom, her open face became a brick.

"Can't fit her in," she said. "Too busy." We left, quickly.

Then, we found Dot. Her busy shop was nestled in another shopping plaza, but when we told her what we needed, she never even blinked. "Come back in ten minutes, and I'll get you set."

After getting some crackers to munch on, we sat on a bench outside the general store, watching the locals walk past with popcorn and live bait. "You sure you want to do this?" I asked her.

Mom turned to me with a look I have known since I was a child—the one that meant we weren't to discuss this anymore. She walked back to the beauty shop as if she were balancing a book on her head.

"You sit down right here," Dot said, patting the chair. Mom took her hat off, and the other women in the shop got quiet. This wasn't the ordinary styling job.

Dot reached for the scissors, and clumps of Mom's hair fell to the polished floor. A close cut was not unusual in this area because Camp Lejeune was nearby, but this was closer than usual for a woman. Dot kept up the cheerful chatter as Mom watched herself change in the mirror.

Next came the shears. Buzzing. Mom's scalp became more clear, white, and covered with little dark short hairs. Exposed, her head looked startling under the light. I held her hand. It was dry and steady.

I stood there awkwardly. I didn't want to look away like there was something I shouldn't see, like catching her in her underwear. Nor did I want to stare. That wouldn't be polite. So, I didn't know what to do with my eyes.

Mom started to get up, but Dot said in a warm voice, "We aren't finished." She gave her a shave, and then a gentle, healing massage. She wasn't afraid of this newly bald head. She touched it, smiled at it, and let Mom know it was okay. She let me know it was okay.

The other women in the shop crowded around. "What beautiful eyes you have," one woman said. "You have a nicely shaped head," another one said. Mom looked around with thanks at the warm greeting her newly sheared head was receiving—a queen collecting tribute. As she stood up and reached for her purse, Dot hugged her and said, "This is my gift to you. Put that away."

Later that day, we walked into a packed restaurant for lunch. We chose a fine one, and it was expensive. As we moved to the bar to wait for our table, a bubble of silence moved with us.

"The diagnosis enters the room before me, " she said as she patted the scarf on her head.

"I noticed," I said out loud, as I silently cursed the other people in the room.

Many women who go though chemo say that losing their hair is one of the hardest parts. I could understand why. Otherwise, they could move through the world undetected. Otherwise, they would still look the same as they did before they had cancer. Otherwise, they could still be themselves. My mom was a woman who had cancer. Not an identity she could embrace easily, I imagined.

Later, back at the trailer, Mom leaped out of the bathroom in a T-shirt, arms curled upward to show off her powerful biceps.

"Do I look like Demi Moore in *GI Jane*?"

"You do, Mom. You sure do."

Amy Hudock

Valentine Power

Do all things with love.

Og Mandino

All through the second grade, I looked forward to grade three. Miss Braun would be my new teacher, and I would finally have a classroom on the main floor of the school, instead of the daylight basement that housed grades one and two. What a huge step up that would be. Best of all, I would be near my best friend, Kate.

Kate, although only three months my elder, was a grade ahead. I missed our daily companionship terribly when she was promoted from the basement to the third grade, but we walked to school together every day and lingered in the hall together until class time. Every recess she would come to my room, or else I would go to hers, and we spent the time together doing best friend things. Early in the term, however, I began to avoid her room because of a bully named David.

David was big for his age and used his size to terrorize younger students—namely, me. His quick wit supplied him with endless caustic remarks and hurtful jibes, which

I tried desperately, but without success, to ignore.

In those days, teachers spent their break time in the staff room, while the students played joyously in the classrooms, down the hallways, or, in nice weather, spilled onto the playground. The boys often played marbles in the aisles between the desks while girls played hopscotch on chalked grids on the oiled floor. Games of dodge ball, floor hockey, or pig-in-the-middle were played in the wide corridor. Only occasionally would a teacher, or, heaven forbid, the principal, emerge to oversee a few minutes of playtime. Fortunately, there was seldom any misbehavior, unless you count the carefully worded banter bullies used to scare the most timid. Even though I tried to keep an eye out for him, David caught me off guard regularly and delighted at my resulting pain.

In the evenings, while doing dishes together, I often discussed my joys and sorrows with my mother, and talk of my nemesis came up regularly. She usually knew just what to say, and I was reassured by her support and love. However, I doubted her assurance that he "would grow up one day."

One evening, early in February, Mom surprised me with what she called a "surefire solution" to my David problem, and I sat in stunned silence, not believing my ears. "Give him a valentine," she said. My mind raced. *Give him a valentine? I'd rather die. Wait, I would die.* Having lost considerable faith in my mother's wisdom, I quickly pushed the idea aside.

Every year, the students in each classroom decorated a beautiful valentine box with a slot in the lid. The special box ceremoniously stood in a place of honor on the teacher's desk, and for weeks we prepared our valentines and dropped them into the slot for the teacher to distribute during the traditional Valentine's Day party. I always slaved over my valentines, choosing just the right one for my teacher and one for each of my classmates. My mother was insistent that if I gave to one, I gave to all. Of course, that only meant my own classmates. After that I could give to whomever I chose, and I deliberated long and hard that year.

On the morning of February fourteenth, I crossed the hall with trepidation, clutching two cards, one for Kate and one for David. As usual, he accosted me at the threshold, growling at me to get out, but Kate came to my rescue, and I was able to sidestep him. It was a long walk to the front of the room, and after making my deposit in their classroom's valentine box, I turned to plan my escape. Much to my relief, David was absorbed in a marble match on the floor, and Kate still stood guard, just in case. Smiling my gratitude, I quickly retreated.

During the afternoon party I worried, knowing that I had erred. I should never have succumbed to my mother's lapse of reason. But it was too late, and I just knew I would be the laughingstock of the entire school. I scarcely read the valentines that were delivered to me. Even the arrows through the heart-shaped cupcakes with fluffy pink frosting failed to pierce the heavy black cloud that enveloped me.

When the bell rang, I aimlessly followed the crowd into the hallway. As I rounded the corner of the mudroom, my eyes locked with David's. I choked back tears and held my breath, awaiting the inevitable onslaught. He just gave me a strange look and, to my horror, fell into step beside me. I thought to myself, *What a fix! What now?* But fortunately, another boy challenged him to a footrace, and David was off.

As I look back, I have to admit, my mother and Saint Valentine were right.

Lyn Larsen

Mother of Pearls

Wisdom begins in wonder.

Socrates

I was walking in the mall one day with my youngest son, Alec. He was an eight-year-old tycoon in the making. I could already see in those bright, blue eyes of his that he had an incredible reckoning for business and finance. Being a single, working mother raising two boys on one salary, I appreciated his dreams of fortune and his positive outlook for the future.

He holds a lot of dreams dear to his heart, one of which is to own a castle by the sea. I have always told him that if he can see it, he can be it. He made a list of things that he would like to have by the time he reached the century mark, and not all of them were monetary. He wants his children to go to college, to be a grandfather, and that his mother "still lives."

He is a young man with a plan, and hopefully a lot of vitamins and oxygen if he hopes to keep me alive until he's one hundred years of age. I admire his ambition. I love his determination. More than anything in this world,

Alec wants to be a veterinarian, and what matters to him even more than material wealth is helping animals and the people who love them. As Alec and I were walking through the mall together on that seemingly ordinary afternoon, a jewelry store window caught my eye.

There against a blanket of royal blue velvet were shimmering diamonds and glimmering sapphires that would make a queen blush. There were platinum rings with rocks the size of Gibraltar clung to them and sapphires dripping from 24-karat gold necklaces. But in the middle of it all, the gem that caught my eye was a beautiful strand of lustrous pearls. It was subtle in its elegance and it was a whisper—a mere rumor—of what motherhood meant to me.

When I was married, my husband gave me diamond rings and earrings like they were candy, but they were taken away from me just as easily as they were given. Not that I have anything against them, of course, but diamonds never afforded me much happiness. The way I see it, pearls symbolize the milk of motherhood. Every mother should have a strand of genuine pearls around her neck. Just as the pearl is formed around a grain of sand, a mother is formed around the grain of her life and the children in it. She has a way about her that can smooth those rough edges in her life and make her world a better place to be.

My eyes admired the strand of beautiful pearls for a moment, and suddenly I felt a tug at my shirt. "What are you looking at, mom?" Alec asked.

I humbly pointed at the precious necklace in the window. "Isn't it beautiful?" I asked him with a smile.

"Why don't you buy it?" he replied plainly. It sounded good, but he could tell by the look in my eyes that it wouldn't make its way home around my neck, not on that particular day; what was written on that price tag and what was written in the balance of my checkbook were a long way off from ever meeting in person.

"Maybe someday," I breathed heavily. I felt his small, warm hand slip into mine and with a squeeze he said, "I have fifteen dollars to buy it for you."

I couldn't resist kissing the top of his golden locks. "Honey, it costs a lot of money," I said in the whisper of my kiss.

"Well, I'm going to buy it for you when I'm a vet, Mom," he said proudly. I looked at my little boy as he gazed up at me with those big, blue eyes.

"I would love that, almost as much as I love you," I whispered, embracing the sentiment.

I had no doubt that Alec would one day purchase a beautiful strand of pearls for me. I knew him and his determination well enough to understand that he would never forget that day at the mall or the marvel that he witnessed in my eyes.

As we stood there holding hands, I realized that the real pearls I would receive as a mother were not to be found in a jewelry case window, pillowed by blue velvet and pricey price tags. They would be pearls of wisdom and reflection pillowed by the simple, subtle elegance of my life. I would discover them in the most unexpected corners of my son's heart and in the warmth of his hand in mine. I would find them deep in the blue ocean of his eyes and in the sweet calm of his slumber.

I am the mother of two extraordinary boys, and there are pearls beyond a king's ransom to be found in the midst of raising them. And anyone who is raising boys knows that with boys comes lots of sand to form such pearls in a mother's life—some of which has mysteriously made its way between the sheets of my bed, and still no one has claimed the blame. And yet I find it an gift utter to know that having sand in my bed means I have those boys in my life. I am a wealthy woman beyond my dreams, even though I may not always have a checkbook that balances to the penny at the end of each month, nor the money to make such a delightful and frivolous purchase as the beautiful pearl necklace in that store window. But I am happy beyond my means. This I know for sure.

And through the eyes of my children I can see that I, their mother, am a pearl. I am a priceless gem that is adored and occasionally appreciated in a way that would make any queen blush. Over the years, like the pearl, my edges have become round, smooth, and beautiful. Being a single mother can often leave you feeling stranded, but if you look carefully you will find some pearls of your own along the way. Wear them proudly, because they are not only beautiful, they are priceless.

Natalie June Reilly

With Both Ears

Alone we can do so little; together we can do so much.

Helen Keller

Before I had children, I had images of exactly what kind of mother I would be. I would be loving and patient twenty-four hours a day, and I would never yell at my children. I would say things like, "I love you more than life itself," and "I thank God for giving you to me," and "You are the most precious thing in my world." This was my ideal.

Reality came in December of 1998 in the form of a seven-pound, two-ounce baby boy. I found out rather quickly that I was not the perfect mother I had envisioned. I sometimes became frustrated with my screaming newborn. I was often exhausted. I longed to keep my shirt on for more than thirty minutes at a time. But all of this was worth the moments when I magically transformed into the mother I wanted to be. I remember burying my face in his neck and inhaling that delicious, yet indescribable, baby smell. As I dried off his tiny body after a bath, I would whisper, "You are the light in my life, the best thing that ever happened to me." It was these moments that I cherished above all others. I was the mother that my perfect little baby deserved to have.

A few short years later, I was blessed with my second child, a daughter this time. Again, I imagined myself as some kind of mothering goddess who was above impatience and selfishness, who always put her children's needs first. Once again, I was often disappointed that my reality differed so vastly from my ideal. But still, there were those moments I valued more than diamonds. As my daughter nursed, I would gaze down at her and whisper, "My precious baby girl, I absolutely adore you." I would gently rock her to sleep and hold her long after she had dozed off. Then came those amazing milestone moments. The first time she smiled with recognition in her eyes, the first time she returned a love pat on the back, and hundreds of other small, but unforgettable, moments.

The baby years are gone for me now. My daughter is a walking, talking toddler, and my son is gearing up for kindergarten. Those snuggly, precious times are now less frequent, but they still happen. It seems that we are always on the go these days. I am saddened to realize the phrase I utter more than any other is no longer, "I love you," but "Wait just a minute, sweetheart." I say it to my son while I'm changing his sister's diaper; I say it to my daughter while I'm helping her brother practice writing his name. I even say it to my poor husband. I use that phrase, and variations of the same, constantly.

A few weeks ago, my son asked for a snack and I, of course, said, "Give me just a second, honey." I hurried to finish what I was doing and then fixed his snack. He sat down at the table and began to eat. I thought about resuming the task at hand and then decided to sit down with him instead.

"Thanks for waiting for your snack until I finished the dishes. You were very patient."

He nodded and continued to shove peanut butter and jelly into his mouth.

"You know, Jordan, I have been really busy lately. It seems like I am always asking you to wait for what you want. Do you understand why you have to wait sometimes?"

He looked at me funny. "Yes. You say, 'Just a second, Jordan' so you can hear me with both ears. If I talked to you while you were busy with something else, you would only be able to hear me with one ear. But because I wait patiently, I get both your ears at the same time." He nodded at me solemnly.

I was floored. This not quite five-year-old little boy had it all figured out. Even when I said, "Wait a minute," my son heard it as a loving phrase. He heard, "Wait a minute, so I can give you my full attention." He heard, "What you are about to say is important to me, and I want to hear it with both ears."

"Jordan, you are absolutely right," I answered. "I love you so much, and I really like being with you. I want to hear what you have to say with both ears, because you are so important to me." I got up and gave him a tight hug.

I realized an important lesson that day, one that my son already knew. Kids don't need perfection; they don't need a mothering goddess. They need to know that we love them all the time, no matter what. Those amazing "I will love you forever" moments are wonderful, and we need to have them with our children, but they simply cannot happen twenty-four hours a day. But everything we say and do can communicate our feelings if we do it with love.

That night, as I was putting Jordan to bed, he grabbed my face and began turning it from side to side. He was blowing in my ears. That wasn't a form of affection we had used before, so I gave him a strange look.

"I was making sure your ears were all cleaned out, Mom." He pulled me down close to him and whispered in my ear, "I wanted to be sure that both ears could hear me say that I love you bigger than the whole world."

I had tears in my eyes as I answered him. "Oh, honey, I love you bigger than the whole world, too."

"And then some," his little voice confirmed.

Diane Stark

6

ON WISDOM

The more sand that has escaped from the hourglass of our life, the clearer we should see through it.

Jean Paul

Even Exchanges

It's what you learn after you know it all that counts.

John Wooden

I have found that being a mom is all about exchanges. Sometimes the exchange doesn't quite seem fair, yet at other times I have made an exchange that is so far in my favor that I know that God is watching over all of us moms, helping us to balance the scales. He helps to ease the pain of the unfavorable exchanges by blessing us with more than we could ever imagine when we become mothers.

Some of the exchanges elicit a sigh as I longingly remember the way things used to be. As a mom, I've exchanged deep, uninterrupted sleep for recurrent late-night nursing sessions with a newborn. I've traded in the flashy, two-door convertible for a sensible, no-nonsense minivan. I've exchanged a firm, smooth stomach for a little extra jiggle adorned with stretch marks. The sexy little string bikini has been swapped for a one-piece swimsuit with attached skirt. My spotless walls are now decorated with peanut butter and jelly fingerprints. I've replaced candlelit, romantic dinners for two with bright, noisy dinners for four in restaurants that serve toys with their meals. My perfectly styled hair has been switched to a quick pull-it-all-out-of-my-face-didn't-have-time-for-a-shower ponytail. My cute little Gucci handbag has been switched with a mammoth diaper bag.

Other exchanges cause me to pause and take in the wonder of it all and realize how grateful I am to be a part of the sisterhood of moms. For example, I've exchanged my commonplace view of the world for the wonder and excitement of seeing everything for the first time through my child's eyes. My serious personality has been transformed into a fun-loving temperament with a knack for making up silly songs and dances that make my child smile when she is hurt or sad. I have traded my rigid, structured routine with a spontaneity that allows time for an extra story at bedtime and one more hug. My constant rushing and hurriedness have been replaced by a slower pace that allows time to stop and catch a firefly or pick a dandelion. My materialistic priorities have been substituted with a knowledge of what truly matters in this world—health and family. And of course, most important of all, I have exchanged my self-centered heart with a heart that overflows with more love, care, and concern for another human being than I ever thought possible.

Truly, as a mom, I am actually making the ultimate exchange: exchanging my self-centered life for a life full of willing sacrifice. I am dedicating my life to caring for and nurturing another human soul that will carry on after I've gone. Now that is an exchange worth making.

Tessa Floehr

"When I was a 'Desperate Housewife,' no one wanted to do a TV show about my life."

Parting Is Sweet Sorrow

You are the bows from which your children as living arrows are sent forth.

Kahlil Gibran

I stood outside the door holding little Adam tightly on one hip, a diaper bag slung over my other shoulder. I peered through the glass at the other mothers dropping off their kids and repeated to myself, *I can do this. I can do this.*

After a few moments of an internal pep talk, another mother came out the door and held it open for me. I went through it—a small step for Adam, a giant leap for his reluctant mother.

I had been both looking forward to and dreading this first day of the Mother's Day Out program at church. The thought of a day to myself was wildly appealing, but somehow tainted by the thought of leaving behind twenty-one-month-old Adam. Sure, I've left him before, but always with either a grandparent or a trusted baby-sitter and only for a few hours. Somehow this felt different. At the Mother's Day Out program, he would be one of several needy toddlers, and he wouldn't be surrounded by the familiar comforts of home.

Still holding tightly to my son, I slowly walked down the corridor until I came to his classroom. Because I was over an hour late, the program director looked up, smiled, and said, "We weren't sure if you were coming today or not."

"We're running a little late this morning," I replied. Little did she know I'd purposefully dawdled all morning trying to talk myself out of bringing him. But deep down I knew it was time—time for Adam to have one day a week to spend playing with other kids, learning new things, growing his independence, and time for me to learn the art of letting go, a little at a time. But the baseball-sized lump in my throat told me it was definitely not going to be easy.

Babies are physically separated from their mothers moments after birth, when fathers traditionally cut the cord. But the true connection—that pure love and devotion we feel for our children—is a tie that is never severed. A mother always feels like her child is very much a part of who she is.

So there I was, standing in the church nursery about to hand my heart over to a group of people I'd just met. Sure, I'd checked out the program, asked lots of questions, and had heard good things about it from other parents. But how could I be sure that everything would be okay?

I introduced Adam to the teachers and handed over his diaper bag. I rattled off a dozen random facts I thought they needed to know—Adam's penchant for climbing tall, dangerous objects and his tendency to cram too many cereal bars in his mouth. They both had kind faces and were mothers themselves, nodding their heads as if they completely understood my nervousness.

I crouched down and put Adam on the floor with a half-dozen other toddlers who were engrossed in a Barney video. I knew it was best to make the good-bye clean and quick, to minimize any negative reaction. So with a hug and a promise to return, I headed for the door, knowing that if I thought about it a moment longer, I might change my mind.

In the end, one of us did cry on the first day of Mother's Day Out, but it wasn't the one wearing the diaper. Perhaps Adam decided to be the strong one so his clingy mother could muster the will to walk out the door. Or maybe he was just more interested in the Barney video than in his mother's melodramatic departure. Whatever the reason, I made it to the car, wiping big tears away as I drove off. In that moment, I realized how tough it is for parents who must work to make this daily decision to leave their child.

I spent the day hurrying from one errand to the next, keeping myself busy so the time would go quickly. Several times I glanced back at the empty car seat and felt an ache in my chest. At the mall, I heard every cry and coo of every baby within fifty yards. All day I fought the feeling that I'd forgotten something very important, as if I'd left my right arm behind.

Finally, the time came to pick him up, and I nearly ran from the parking lot to the door. The mother and child reunion was joyous indeed. Adam came running into my arms, and I hugged him harder than ever before. The teachers said he had done beautifully all day and even wrote "wonderful behavior" on his report card. I beamed with pride as I carried him out to the car.

Despite my internal drama, this weekly "day out" is good for both of us. Adam will continue to embrace his individuality, and perhaps I will even learn how to slow down and appreciate the time alone—to read a book, write in silence, and maybe even have an uninterrupted phone conversation. Most of all, this weekly day away reminds me that the time we spend with our children, no matter how long or short, is meant to be treasured.

Gwen Rockwood

The Rocking Chair

It requires wisdom to understand wisdom: the music is nothing if the audience is deaf
Walter Lippmann

A recent, bestselling, self-help book asked, "Think about a time when you felt peaceful and relaxed. Where were you? What were you doing?"

As the mother of two energetic children under the age of five, my knee-jerk response was, "Does the nanosecond between falling into bed and my head hitting the pillow in a dead sleep count?" Later, while rocking my toddler to sleep, I pondered the question again. I couldn't remember a time since becoming an adult (and especially a mother) when I felt totally at ease, peaceful, and relaxed. This was disturbing. Was I always in overdrive, running at full speed, but going nowhere?

Probably the closest I ever got to this state was the occasional evening. The dishes were done. Everything was prepped for the next day. I didn't have lesson plans, bills, or other pressing projects to do. My preschooler, Katie, was tucked snugly into bed. My husband, Toshi, was in the garage playing his guitar. I sat in the dark of my toddler Andy's room, my feet propped up on the ottoman, rocking him to sleep.

Andy snuggled up to me, pulling my head down with his chubby little hand until we were cheek-to-head. The house was dark and totally quiet. My mind gradually slowed down to the pace of our gentle rocking. Sometimes I mentally planned the next day and occasionally even contemplated deep thoughts. Many times, I was one-step above dozing. Sometimes I even dipped into dreamland.

I sang there: "Edelweiss," "Hush Little Baby," and "Twinkle, Twinkle, Little Star." I prayed there: "The Lord's Prayer" plus my own. I whispered quietly there: telling Andy how much I loved him even though he didn't get as much individual attention as I would have liked. I apologized there: telling Katie how sorry I was for being grumpy and promising to be more patient tomorrow. We discussed tomorrow's events. How Granny would come visit soon. How blessed I was that they were mine.

The rocking chair hasn't always been a positive place. I've fumed there after losing an argument and felt resentful there after a teething baby screamed all night. I've cried there and felt hopeless and overwhelmed there. I have even felt impatient and tied down there. However, these were exceptions, not the norm.

Mostly the chair represents a place where I nourished my children's hearts, minds, and souls. Besides lots of nursing, I rocked a feverish Katie to sleep there and held a chronically congested Andy upright for hours there. I've inspired a love of books in our children by reading stories in our special chair. Even when my belly bulged out with Andy and my lap space grew smaller, Katie crowded on anyway for a story before her afternoon nap. She giggled, as Andy would try to kick her off my lap from in utero.

Last fall we moved to Arizona. It was time to move

Andy into a "big boy" bed and room. We didn't need the rocking chair anymore. Toshi suggested selling it, but I couldn't get rid of it. In the whirlwind of activity related to starting a new life 2,500 miles away from friends and family, I needed a touchstone of tranquility. Somewhere I could sit in the dark and rock with my favorite blankie around my shoulders, somewhere I could sing softly to myself, read, and pray, and somewhere I could nurture my own heart, mind, and soul.

Yes, it clashes with my bedroom décor. It has spit-up stains on it, and I stub my toe on it every time I make my bed. Yet, I can't get rid of it. I plan to keep the rocking chair long after my babies are grown. It will always represent the nourishing of my children and hopefully, of myself, too.

Sara Francis-Fujimura

Someone's Daughter

Long before I had "mom" on my resume, I was some-one's daughter. Of course, I didn't know what being "someone's daughter" truly meant until I had a daughter of my own, Drew.

Before Drew even entered this world, my precious daughter was the unsuspecting vessel for a magnificent bundle of dreams and expectations. I promised myself and my future female progeny that her "story" would be more profound, her list of accomplishments longer, her acts of kindness more abundant, her contributions as a woman, and eventually a mother, better than mine. I pledged to confess my life's lessons and humbling regrets, in hopes that she would learn from my mistakes and tread uncharted grounds and alternative routes along her own journey.

I knew from the beginning that my daughter and I couldn't be more different. From our hair color and com-plexion to our taste in clothes and food, we've continued to contrast like the black and white on a Rorschach test. I joke that Drew should have been my glamorous sister's child; my only daughter came into this world adept at applying makeup, putting together unique clothing ensembles, and choosing the appropriate hair products. I endured premature and heated disagreements about ear piercing, leg shaving, and eyebrow plucking—things my still kickin' Bohemian and pierceless self put off as long as possible.

Don't get me wrong—Drew is all the things any mom could wish for in a daughter. She's intelligent, beautiful, creative, and kind. She's passionate, compassionate, sports a sarcastic wit (okay, that's one trait we share), is not afraid of hard work, and takes pride in a job well done.

I've witnessed her question the world around her, stand up for what she thinks is right, and bulldoze her way down a soccer field. I've also viewed the little girl asleep in her bed with all her innocence intact. I've observed the tooth fairy losing its mystique and nursery rhymes losing their appeal. I've noted the transition from inquisitive little girl to introspective and contemplative adolescent. I've seen face value replaced with conclusions of her own. I've beheld her all dressed for her first dance while trying to contain my pounding heart. I've managed to endure and forgive when she stomped on that heart once or twice. I've watched her long coltlike legs carry her across the gymnasium's wood floor to retrieve her elementary school diploma with all the confidence of someone twice her age. I've been there also to see her weep over things not in her control and rejoice when she's triumphed over the odds.

I've held her head and hand in sickness, and I've told her stories to occupy her mind while she's waited at the dentist. I've discussed the inexplicable tragedies in the news and enlightened her on the facts of life. I've bit my tongue for her own good when I watched her make the wrong choice and remained relatively calm while allowing her to come to the right alternative.

She's trusted me to protect her, shelter her, and nourish her growth. She's counted on me to run defense when others have let her down. She's accepted my powers to chase away bad dreams and bullies, soothe broken hearts, and explain unfairness as best I can. She's allowed me to learn as I go in this motherhood role and understood when I sometimes fell short. She's seen me at my best, and certainly my worst, and loves me unconditionally in spite of it all.

Drew is sometimes a mirror reflecting fleeting moments of my own youth and sometimes a crystal ball when I get glimpses of the woman she'll one day become. My only daughter will, hopefully, one day have a daughter of her own and understand the depth and breadth of my love for her, and the limitless and immeasurable ways she fulfills my life.

Being someone's daughter is a blessing. Having a daughter is beyond compare.

Lori Shaw-Cohen

Never Save the Best for Last

The joy that isn't shared dies young.

Anne Sexton

Instead of New Year's Eve, I make resolutions on my birthdays. It seems somehow more quiet and personal.

This year I decided it was time to sell or donate my mother's possessions that no one in the family was planning on using. Those boxes in the attic had uncomfortably loomed over me for five years.

The bittersweet process didn't go as I expected. As I stumbled through the carton-crammed attic, the first box I opened held my mother's sterling silver flatware, and wedged inside was her favorite evening purse, wrapped in blue felt. A tiny beauty, with pale peach roses embroidered on beige satin and a handle dotted with pearls and emeralds, the purse could fit in my palm. I couldn't imagine ever carrying it myself when going out to dinner, but maybe someday I'd find an evening worthy of its elegance. So I put it in my pocket to save, as Mom used to say, "for best."

As I hid the treasure in my pocket, memories washed

over me from when I was little. When I was sick, I was allowed to go through Mother's jewelry drawers. I loved pulling out costume diamond brooches and clip-on earrings. Peering in her vanity mirror, I made up stories about wearing them. That's also where she kept her little purses. I always completed my fantasies by matching one of them to complement my ensemble. And my favorite was the one now in my pocket.

Behind the silverware were stacks of tightly sealed cartons—cartons that I hadn't been able to face in the years since she died, boxes that I so quickly, efficiently, and hold-on-tight emotionlessly packed up the week after her funeral. With a rich sadness, I peeled the tape off of one. It held pastel blue Wedgwood china with raised white bands of grapevines around the edges. It was in museum-quality condition because it had never been used.

Then I found a set of crystal that sparkled with brilliant diamond clarity. Tumblers and candlesticks and a huge cut glass punch bowl. I carefully unwrapped a Waterford vase. *How come I never saw any of this?* I thought. The vase was a metaphor for her life. A daughter of penniless Russian immigrants, my mother grew up proudly able to afford good crystal. But she couldn't allow herself the joy of using it. Like many unclaimed joys in her life, she saved it for "best." And more often than not, best never came.

I think that was why I was too afraid to let myself think about the things I packed after she died. It was too sad to see wine glasses that never glistened on a lace tablecloth and china that was perfect because no one ever put a slice of cake on it.

Later, as I set the table for my beloved yearly birthday lasagna bash, I flirted with using my mother's handmade white embroidered tablecloth, but I pictured it with the resulting tomato sauce stains and changed my mind. My husband softly admonished me. "You might as well throw it out if you're going to keep it in the attic. Why have it take up space?" So with gleeful abandon, I unfurled the pristine white tablecloth and set the table for seven people who arrived soon afterward, dressed in party attire.

I believe that had my mother known she would never even take a sip of water from her beautiful crystal tumbler, or never put a bouquet of her home-grown roses in her lovely Waterford vase, she would have been heartbreakingly sad. Because of that, not one of my mother's treasured belongings would be taken out of my house.

And so, as I turned the corner of another birthday, I made a new resolution. I didn't want someone in the next generation to go through my attic and find treasures I've never used. What on earth would be the point in that? If something breaks, it breaks. My new motto? Use the good stuff!

My guests and I laughed our way through dinner, and nobody spilled sauce on the tablecloth. Instead, I knocked over an entire glass of red wine. I was horrified, but I bet Mom wouldn't have minded one bit. I think she would have loved that ruby-red stain. I wish she could have been there to celebrate with me. She would have adored how her favorite purse matched my peach satin blouse.

Saralee Perel

A Good Call

I want this to be a good telephone call, I said to myself. My son Steve was on the phone. I hadn't seen him in a while, and I missed him. I wanted to see his face in front of me. I wanted to put my arms around him, as if he were a little boy again. I wanted to tell him that even though he was a grown man, the mother in me comes alive when we are together.

But I wanted this to be a good call. No pressure. No guilt. No whining. He lives away from home. There were no children left for me to tend. The bedrooms were now empty, but I still thought of his bedroom as his.

I remembered calling my parents after I left home. Sometimes the calls weren't good. I would hang up feeling guilty about this or that, not visiting enough, not calling enough, not doing one thing or another enough. I promised myself I would not do that to my children. After all, I was a liberated woman, a mother of the nineties, much more aware, more sensitized, more independent then those of yesteryear. I had a career, a healthy support group of friends. I drove my own car. I knew better than to complain.

So I wanted this to be a good call. I talked about the

weather, about my work, about his job, about any interesting topics of the day. I tried to be pleasant and pushed down the words, "I miss you." I suffocated the plea, "I need to see you." I kept silent the complaint, "Of course, I know you're busy, but I truly don't care. I want to see your face like I want to see tomorrow's sunrise, or like I need to breathe."

I wanted this to be a good call, yet there were fears that have slept with me all night. The rooms were too empty. The walls still echoed of stories told to my young children years ago. Could my son tell me something to make me feel better? He was young and filled with energy for the future. Perhaps he could share some of it with me? Oh, how nice it would be if I could sit across from him. Perhaps then nothing might need be said, as his presence would be enough.

The words fought with me, and I felt them winning, but I wanted this to be a good call. I know all the reasons I shouldn't say what I wanted to say. I know it is natural for children to leave their parents. I realize it's the way it's supposed to be, that they form their own lives. I was going to be a today's woman, self-sufficient, needing nothing but my ability to make it on my own two feet.

But I've run out of strength and resolve. The call had lasted too long. My self-control was ebbing. "I miss you," I wailed into the telephone. "How long do I have to wait until I see your face?"

Just like any mother from the beginning of time.

Harriet May Savitz

The Best Choice

If there were dreams to sell, what would you buy?

T. L. Beddoes

Choices—it's what life is all about. Some are seemingly insignificant, while others are monumental. And sometimes, as I have learned, choices made in the toughest of circumstances can turn out to be very positive life-changers.

At twenty-seven, I figured I had made a lot of good choices up to that point in life. I chose a career that was in high demand and offered a comfortable income, and I chose to marry my high school sweetheart. Together, we chose to raise our "textbook" family (one boy and one girl) in the rural mountains far from the chaos of city life—not a terribly difficult choice, even though we had to make some sacrifices to make it all happen. I thought I was generally in control of my life by the choices I had made, but then something happened that was completely out of my control, and the choices became more difficult: our seven-week-old son died of sudden infant death syndrome.

This can't be happening, I told myself. Never would I have chosen to experience something like this. In my carefully planned and executed life this kind of tragedy didn't fit anywhere. It was my worst nightmare. There was no logical explanation for this kind of loss. There was nothing I could have done to prevent it, and it left me feeling completely out of control. Overnight, my world had been turned upside down without any warning.

It wasn't that I was unfamiliar with death (both of my parents died during my childhood), but I had never before held death in my arms, stroked its soft hair or kissed its lifeless face. Parents die; children do not. This was an unnatural and unwanted intrusion into my perfectly ordered world, and I was devastated. I didn't choose it. I didn't want it. But the funeral director told my husband and me something on that fateful morning that made a huge difference in our lives. With hands folded and a sober expression on his face, he told us quite candidly, "Statistics show the biggest aftermath from the loss of a child is the break-up of the marriage. If you don't work hard to keep your lines of communication open, you'll risk being among those statistics."

Dealing with the death of a child was monumental enough. I didn't want to face the death of a marriage as well. I knew that even the best of marriages could crumble without adequate maintenance, so I made a choice right then to do whatever it took to keep our marriage strong. It wasn't always easy: we were often on an emotional seesaw, one of us up, the other down. It's hard to offer each other support when you are both grieving the loss of a child. But every morning, before I got out of bed, I made the choice to be as supportive of my husband as I could be and to ask others for support on those days when I had none to give. I chose not to let the horrible pain I felt inside cripple my relationship with either my husband or our three-year-old daughter. Even though I might not be in control of things that happened to me, I could still be in control of how I reacted.

Fortunately, my husband made the same choice, and we worked hard at communicating more deeply than ever before. And together we chose to try again, even though we knew there was always the same risk with every child.

When our subsequent son was born just thirteen months later, I had even more difficult choices to make. It quickly became obvious that standing over his crib or keeping him in my sight twenty-four hours a day was not a viable option. I knew that ultimately I could not control whether he lived or died, so I looked beyond myself and chose to trust God with things that were beyond my control. It's the best choice I've ever made.

Not long ago, my now twenty-seven-year-old son, the one whose crib I eventually had to stop watching over, asked me how I manage to seem so "normal" considering some of things I've endured in my life.

"It's not that hard," I told him. "It's all about choices. You can choose to be a victim or a victor. I just chose the latter."

Caroleah Johnson

In My Other Life

In my other life, I used to stay up late. When I finally went to bed, it was wearing a nice nightgown—not a stained T-shirt and boxers.

In my other life, the numbers were lower for my weight, my cholesterol, and my blood pressure. I was fine just eating a salad with a glass of wine for dinner.

In my other life, I exercised by taking long hikes up the mountain and watched the sunset. I didn't have to hurry home to get dinner ready. The meal I prepared did not have to be palatable for anyone's taste buds but mine. At the parties I hosted, I served gourmet appetizers and cocktails. There were no paper hats or cupcakes involved. I stayed up until 3:00 AM, knowing I could sleep in the next morning. In my other life, sleeping in did not mean getting up at 7:30 AM.

In my other life, my house and car were immaculate. I never had Cheerios hidden under car seats, used tissues stuffed into the side pockets of the backseat, or melted crayons smashed into the rug. I also never had the pleasure of finding a lost sippy cup containing green, congealed milk.

In my other life, my clothes were trendy and plentiful.

There were no stains from sticky fingers or magic marker on my best shirt. My hair was cut every six weeks, my fingernails were polished, and I did not wear closed shoes in the summer to hide my unpedicured toes. I only had to worry about brushing my own teeth and cleaning my own ears. I did not have to worry about the cleanliness of someone else's body parts. I actually had extra money in my bank account that could be used to pay for luxuries for myself. I replaced my shoes before they fell apart. My paycheck was not sucked dry by daycare payments. Extra money did not go toward swimming lessons or babysitters.

In my other life, I could read a book from cover to cover without interruptions. The books I read did not contain pictures on every page or involve any of the Disney princesses.

In my other life, I saw movies in the theater. I made sure to see all the award-nominated films before the Oscars premiered. I stayed until the end of the show. I even watched the credits! There was no worry of how much this additional time in the dark would cost me when it was time to pay the babysitter. I felt sorry for the people who had to rent the summer blockbuster in late fall and watch it on a small-screen television. Didn't they realize the whole experience was better if you had surround sound while sharing buttered popcorn with your date?

In my other life, I did things like lingering over a cup of tea with a friend in a coffee house. I knew the best places for happy hour and was friendly with the bartenders who gave ladies free drinks. I went to restaurants that did not provide crayons to color on the paper tablecloth. If I came to work tired, it was because of the previous evening's fun, not because I was in a steamy shower trying to get a toddler to stop coughing. My desk at work had pictures from my latest exotic vacation, pictures in which I was holding a drink in at least one hand. I planned future vacations to places that did not feature a "Kids Club" or have "babysitters available on request."

In my other life, I didn't go to zoos on the weekend or look for discount coupons for the circus. I did not know who the Wiggles were, much less get upset when I found out one of them was ill and had to retire.

Would I go back to "my other life"? Not in a million years.

My car was clean but I never had the joy of wiping away tiny fingerprints that made a picture on a steamy window. If I was stuck at a red light, I wouldn't say the rhyme my father taught me as a child, "Red light, red light, turn to green, by the count of three, or I shall scream." My father died when I was seven and somehow saying this rhyme with the granddaughter he never met makes me feel closer to him. I play "punch bug" with my daughter on the way to school, and we both get excited as a VW Beetle comes into view.

My hair may not be stylish, but when I put it in a ponytail to keep it out of my eyes, my daughter tells me I look like a princess. And my shoes may be worn or out of style, but they delight my daughter as she prances around in them, pretending she's wearing Cinderella's slippers.

My fridge has a portrait of me drawn in purple finger paint because my daughter knows it's my favorite color. I may not be able to read the latest novel, but I have passed on my love of books and theater to my daughter. She gives a different voice to each one of the three bears as we read the adventures of Goldilocks. I've learned buttered popcorn tastes just as good watching television in my basement and sharing it with little, sticky fingers.

My exotic vacations have become places for "family fun," rather than dancing, snorkeling, or rum cruises. I'm certain my husband and I had as much fun as our daughter did when we visited the Magic Kingdom. And I've visited a barnyard zoo on Mother's Day and milked a cow. I actually made her moo. I'm pretty sure it's because I was a breastfeeding mother.

I don't go to bars to flirt or meet a handsome stranger, because my husband will gladly sit on our deck with me and share a bottle of wine. Occasionally, we do treat ourselves for some alone time over dinner, where we mostly talk about how much we love our daughter and discuss our hopes and dreams for her. Once home, and the sitter gone, we check on our daughter as she is sleeping and kiss her good night.

My desk now has pictures of my family on it. These photos serve as a reminder of what is really important. The photos remind me that no one was ever on their deathbed wishing they spent more time at the office.

I'd never go back to my other life. If I did, I'd give up the best thing I've ever done in this one . . . becoming a mom.

Kathryn Veliky

I Remember Mama

The fragrance always stays in the hand that gives the rose.

Hada Bejar

The closet smelled like Mama.

My mother died when I was ten. For some reason, the closet in my father's bedroom still had all her clothes in it. I don't know why he didn't get rid of them. Was it that the grief was so raw that he couldn't bring himself to do it, or with five girls in the family to raise, did economy dictate the clothes were still wearable?

I also don't know why I went into the closet that day, but I did. My father's room was his inner sanctum, and I rarely stepped across its threshold except to clean it. I wasn't there to clean when I went into the closet. I walked through the door, and there she was. My mother. Her presence came back to me with as much substance as if she'd been hiding in the darkness. It was her smell. I felt as if it had been waiting for me, hanging in the air of that tiny room, giving me time to grieve and come to terms with life.

I didn't realize people had individual smells. It wasn't a perfume smell, although there was the shadow of Evening in Paris mixed with the uniqueness that I smelled each time she hugged me. I'd given her that bottle of perfume for Mother's Day. She looked so surprised and happy when she opened it that I knew it was the most precious thing I could spend my meager savings on. A whole year after she was gone, after I admitted she was dead, after I stood tearless and numb before her grave and realized I would never again see her or hear her voice, there she was now, alive in my memory.

They say the sense of smell is the most potent for recalling memory. At eleven I learned the truth of this theory. For a moment, I could only stand and take it in, allow it to settle over me like a warm, comfortable blanket. I could see her clearly, in good health, not carrying the pallor of sickness that would take her life. She was without pain, dressed in the blue chemise that I loved and thought she looked best in. She smiled at me, and I could see our lives. It wasn't my life that passed before my eyes, but hers. I remembered us together, not with my sisters and brother, but, selfishly, just the two of us. I clung to the vision, wanting her all to myself. I knew it was only for a short time, and I didn't want to share. There was nothing fantastic in what I saw, at least not to anyone other than myself. I smiled in the darkness as the days passed before me, and the small incidences of life were recalled in bright flashes inside my head. I don't know how long it went on—it seemed like hours, but memory moves at the speed of light. Probably only a few seconds passed, but it was an eleven-year-old lifetime to me.

I pulled one of her coats from its hanger and slipped my arms into it. The smell stayed with me, closer now than it had ever been. I removed the coat from the closet and I wore it until my arms grew longer than the sleeves and my legs hung too many inches below its hem for style to allow. The coat provided protection, not only from the cold Buffalo winters, but from the hurt of life.

Then one day the smell was gone, like the disappearance of the newborn baby smell. I can't tell you when the coat no longer smelled like my mother, just as I don't know when the baby smell goes away. One day it was no longer there, as if it knew I was ready to take on the world under my own terms. I no longer needed the support of my mother. While I knew she would always be with me, the coat had taken on my own unique smell. But I remembered Mama's.

Grief is a hard thing to work through, especially when you're a child and don't understand the intricacies of life and death or why God decided to take away the person you loved more than anyone else in the world. Like the smell of my mother fading and mine taking up its place, the pain went away one day at a time, one layer at a time, and I'd passed from girlhood into an adult woman.

I often wonder who I would be had my mother lived. The path of my life would probably be very different from what it is now, but the thing I do know is that the memories she gave me survived the pain and grief of losing her.

Today I'm a single mom and a grandma. Life is very precious, and spending time with my children is a high priority. With the many demands on my time, I give preference to my children and the events in their lives: dance recitals, school programs, or just a talk in the car. Children grow fast. I work hard to make sure they have the same kind of happy memories my mother left me.

Shirley T. Hailstock

No Longer a Rookie

Few of us go through life without taking part in some kind of rite of passage.

Hank Nuwer

My son Noah was called up to the "Big Show" this year. No baseball scouts, no tryouts. All he had to do was turn nine years old, which he did in October, making him ineligible for the younger Rookie League.

It was time to move up to the Minor Leagues, the Big Time. He was thrilled, because he was now able to wear real baseball socks. As for me? My heart began a slow climb up my chest and into my throat where it has remained for the last several weeks.

You see, I loved the Rookie League. It was still nurturing enough with just the right amount of action. The Rookie League was a welcome oasis from T-ball, which was adorable for about the first two innings of the season but then dragged on like a merry-go-round that wouldn't stop. For a mom who always cried at the end of *The Bad News Bears,* the Rookie League was exactly what baseball should be; every kid got to play every position, and each one coveted the day when they could wear the catcher's gear. There was a pitching machine that only threw strikes, and the hitter got five strikes, not three, before called out. We cheered our kids when they forgot to run, threw to the wrong base, or did the "I-gotta-pee" dance out in left field. There was also a snack schedule.

But the Minors? It was, pardon the expression, a whole new ballgame.

By the time kids made it to the Minor League, the weaker players had mostly dropped out. So while my son was middle of the pack in the Rookie League, he suddenly found himself lacking the prowess and knowledge shared by the other kids. In other words, he was at the end of the batting order and inevitably played the outfield.

Wow, these nine- and ten-year-olds were talented! They could pitch strikes. They could steal bases. They could catch pop flies. Everyone hit. It was no longer fun to be the catcher; it was downright scary. *What were we thinking, throwing our kid into this mix?* I worried to myself. *Oh, that's right—Noah said he wanted to play.*

So I attended each game with fifty percent trepidation and fifty percent prayer. I watched as the boys warmed up on the field, throwing balls to one another. *Thwack! Thwack! Thwack!* My son's glove didn't make that noise. In fact, he caught about one of every five balls. I suddenly and inexplicably hated my husband for not drilling him on how to catch a ball so that it made the "thwack" noise. Then Noah took a rebound off his glove right to the nose—for the third time that season. I watched the tears come to his eyes as he tried to shake it off. I saw him mouth the words "I'm okay" to himself. He kept playing. My heart hurt. I wanted to cry, too. Baseball was fast becoming no longer fun for me. I wondered, *Is it fun for him?*

In my little folding chair, set up with all the other

parents along the first-base line, I listened to the voices in my head. *The coaches are very good and fair.* (Please spend a little extra time with my kid.) *The kids are nice.* (Please don't say anything mean to my boy when he misses the fly ball.) *It's a sunny day.* (Please let a spontaneous storm come along so this can all be over.) But the game went on. It was Noah's turn to bat. *Swing. Strike One. Swing. Strike Two.* The pitcher wound up again and delivered a ball that Noah must have thought was too inside; he cringed and the ball serendipitously hit the bat and dribbled about five feet in front of home plate. Noah just stared at it.

"RUN!" was the collective advice from nearly everyone present.

He did, taking advantage of the fielders who didn't quite know what to do with the accidental bunt. He had a single, and his grin was as wide as ever. With a high-five from coach, Noah did a little dance. I cheered, quickly swallowing the vomit that had risen during the last ten seconds of play.

The inning ended, and Noah cheerfully trotted out to the field. *This was fun for him.* It was then I realized what this particular baseball season was all about. It all made perfect sense; at some point in life, you are rewarded in places where you have talent. I realized that baseball was not going to be Noah's destination, but he was having fun with the journey, despite my misguided instincts to protect him.

But what about this mother's heart? I'm happy to report that it has left my throat and is now out in center field, with Noah. He is every bit a minor leaguer, but his mother will always be a rookie.

Emily Mendell

"Trevor gets his exercise playing baseball.
I get mine running him to games and practice."

7

LETTING GO

*It is good to have an end to journey toward,
but it is the journey that matters in the end.*

Ursula K. LeGuin

Hands-Free

Let your children go if you want to keep them.

Malcolm Forbes

While walking into the grocery store yesterday, I couldn't escape the feeling that something was wrong. I checked my purse for my keys and checkbook. I felt for my sunglasses on top of my head. Everything was accounted for down to the list in my hand, and that's when I realized what was wrong. My hands—no one was holding my hands.

I was shopping without my husband or kids. There was no one to pull me along if I chose to dawdle and no one for me to drag away from the candy aisle (though I must say, now that my husband is forty, he's getting better about not begging for treats).

I sat down on a bench at the end of the checkout line to ponder this feeling of freedom. I haven't had "free" hands since the birth of my oldest son sixteen years ago. When they wheeled me out of the hospital with my precious bundle in my arms, I felt overwhelmed. Then they handed me his diaper bag, my purse, several pots of flowers, a balloon bouquet, and a list of important childcare instructions. I scanned the list. Nowhere did it tell me how to grow an extra pair of hands.

We humans are adaptable creatures. Caring for my son quickly became second nature. When he was two years old, we presented him with a baby brother, and I realized I hadn't even begun to master the art of baby juggling. After some tearful trips to the grocery store, I dried my eyes and bought a baby leash. I could traipse about with a baby in my arms, one tethered to my hand, and an extra-large diaper bag slung over my shoulder.

Soon our second child was walking. The older held my hand and tried to help me rein in his perpetually moving sibling. I finally realized I could leave the diaper bag in the car, and life became more manageable. Then a third child was added to our family.

What to do? Three children and only two hands? I bought an infant front pack, and I now had one hand for my five-year-old to cling to and one hand for the wild toddler who needed at least six hands to contain him.

Finally the glorious day arrived when all three children could walk and were toilet trained. I no longer needed to carry a diaper bag! We all linked hands when we crossed the street, or when we approached the candy aisle of the grocery store. Freedom and free hands were in reach.

Imagine my surprise when I discovered a fourth child was on the way! The juggling routine reappeared with a vengeance. I was astounded by a whole new selection of baby products designed to make a mother's life easier. Sippy cups, disposable bottles, and Snugglies were wonderful, but no matter how clever these conveniences were, they still weren't as helpful an extra pair of hands.

So how did I end up alone at the store with no one pulling on my hands as I pondered the ripeness of the melons, and no one straining at a leash while I sniffed the scented candles?

I blinked, and suddenly my firstborn was sixteen and fully capable of holding down the fort for a few hours while I shopped. I got up to get a cart, and my hands swung listlessly at my sides. I felt incomplete, as if I were missing a limb. I had so longed for the day when my hands would be free again, but now I couldn't remember why.

I looked up to see an elderly woman tottering through the exit toward the congested parking lot. A man about my age appeared at her side. "Here, Mom, take my hand. I can't have you wandering away from me," he said. The woman looked at his outstretched hand and smiling she intertwined her fingers with his.

I have seen the future. It isn't all hands-free, and I'm glad.

Cindy Hval

The Fragrance

Lydia sat on the edge of her bed in her nightgown. As I entered, her large brown eyes sparkled with "life" while death lingered around her. A physical therapist, I had come into her home to help her remain functional as long as possible while she dealt with end-stage cancer. I had been told that her husband suffered dysfunction due to grief over her illness, and only her children could help her.

The expression in Lydia's eyes reminded me of my mother's. Though my mother's eyes were blue, they also had shone with "life" even as life ebbed away. When Mom saw me approach down the nursing home corridor, her eyes spoke that she wanted to jump out of her wheelchair and run to me.

Just as Mom had passed away, soon Lydia would, too, and I wondered if, like Mom, something of Lydia's true inner self behind those gleaming eyes would linger for her children. Such things remained a mystery to me, but still, I hoped.

I sat down on the bed beside Lydia and got acquainted. Due to her condition, very soon she had to use the commode.

"My son, John, will help me." In a twinkling, her teenage

son appeared at her side and adroitly pivoted her onto the commode.

Drawn to her eyes, I noticed a flicker of embarrassment as she made the painful transfer and clung helplessly to her son. In the past, she had been the gracious lady of the house, and this change of destiny, loss of hair and all, cheated her of a portion of her dignity.

I stepped out of the room to give her privacy. Again, she seemed so like my mom. I remembered the times after her slight stroke when Mom looked a bit frustrated because she couldn't speak easily anymore.

"John, you did a masterful job," I said, as he seated Lydia back on the side of the bed as if she were a china doll that might break.

"My brother, Paul, is just as careful," John responded in a quiet tone. "One of us desires to be with Mom at all times."

Desires, I pondered to myself. *What a lovely word for a young man to say regarding his mother.*

Lydia's brown velvet eyes flickered with a touch of self-consciousness about such a fuss being made over her. She had obviously been the kind of mother that fussed over everyone else, saw her boys off for the day with a hearty breakfast, washed their clothes, ironed their shirts, and baked their favorite foods for when they got home after school.

I thought again of my own mother who pampered me. She did not require me to make my bed on school days. She ironed my endless supply of cotton skirts and blouses, and laid out cookies and milk when I got home.

When I returned to Lydia's house on the next visit, her condition had deteriorated, and she stayed in bed. While her eyes glistened like deep pools, she remained quiet, as did John and Paul. Out of their devotion for her, they had already figured out how to care for her every need, the very things I came to teach. Not needed, I slipped out of their little sanctuary.

I knocked a few days later to check up on things . . . no response . . . opened the door, "Hello," and tiptoed to her bedside. Much to my surprise she lay, eyes ever bright, under the covers between her two grown sons—both cuddled up against her as if they would never let her go. Even my presence did not disturb them but caused them to hold on a little tighter—their teenage pride thrown out the window just to be able to cling to their mother one last time.

A tear trickled down my cheek, and I turned away to wipe it off. As an adult, I had cuddled with my mom in her bed at the nursing home before she died, not caring who should come in and see us.

So soft, so warm—one last time.

Lydia passed away just hours before my final visit. Her small home, like the family within, remained quiet, yet the home did not feel empty. A mystifying sweet something— was it an aroma?—lingered in the house.

At first it puzzled me. It reminded me of how my own mother's light perfume would linger even when she had left my room and gone out with Dad. How comforting the aroma made me feel when I was young, like she was still present. And years later, when Mom died, a certain fragrant something about her remained in the atmosphere of my life.

Could it be that when a sainted mother departs this earth, she leaves a fragrance of her love for the children she leaves behind? I believe so. Mother-love, like God's love, is forever.

Margaret Lang

Storing Memories

The children's memorabilia filled two closets in our house, covered the sawhorse in the garage, jammed a utility cupboard, and if something wasn't done soon, were destined next for my side of the bed (my wife, of course, denies this).

With that said, I announced at the dinner table the other night that it was time to consolidate the art projects, awards, holiday cards, grades, and other mementos our son and daughter have brought home since preschool into one central, confined location. "Preferably, Grandma's house," I said.

Since my wife balked at that idea, and because our housing covenants don't allow silos, she agreed to go through the stuff and weed it down until everything fit into one, large, plastic bin. After a few hours of effort, she called the children and me into the room.

"How's it going?" I asked.

"What I want to keep won't all fit into the bin," she said in frustration. "In this pile, I have the ones I want, and in this other pile," she said, pointing to a stack of three things—a tiny slip of paper, an old lunchbox, and a broken toothpick house—"are what I'm willing to throw out."

I put my arm around her. "So you need someone to make an unbiased decision of what must go?"

"No, I need a larger bin."

I rummaged around in the "keep" stack. "Well, honey, this can certainly go."

"Wait!" she shouted, snatching the paper away from me. She studied it for a few moments. "Ken, we can't throw that out."

"You want to save our son's spelling test?"

"Of course, it's precious," she replied.

"He got a D-minus."

"I know," she said, pointing at the sheet. "But look at the nice thing the teacher wrote on it."

I studied the paper. "It says, 'nice improvement.'"

"See," she said, carefully placing it in the bin.

My son poked his head over the large pile. "What about this?"

My wife's face broke out into a silly grin. "Oh, I don't think I can really let that one go," she said, pulling down to her heart the macaroni necklace our daughter made a few years ago in kindergarten. "I wore this to the Country Club Dinner/Dance."

"You went into public with it?" my daughter said disgustedly.

"Of course I did—you asked me to." She turned to me. "Remember what the waiter said?"

"No."

She smiled giddily at the children. "He said the pasta really brought out my eyes."

Our daughter grabbed the necklace. "Hey! Why do four of the noodles look cooked?"

My wife frowned. "They dipped in my soup."

We went back and forth over twenty-five more things, each one landing back in the "keep" pile until I finally gave up. "Why don't you put everything back where it was—it's obvious you aren't ready for this. "

"I can keep all of it?" she asked.

"Yes."

She held up the tiny slip of paper in the discard pile. "Even our son's first bicycle lock combination?"

I nodded. "I suppose I could always sleep on the couch."

Ken Swarner

Filling the Gap

Love builds bridges where there are none.

R. H. Delaney

Her name was Kim Lorraine, and in the spring of 1956, she died moments after she tiptoed into this world. She was laid to rest in France, where my family was stationed at the time. Kim was my sister.

No one knew the real cause of death, just that she had a very small head, and life would have been a brutal challenge had she lived. When the doctor detected abnormalities during Mom's pregnancy, he confided his diagnosis to my father, adding that the baby would either be stillborn or not live very long. It was recommended that Dad keep the diagnosis to himself, because the doctor did not want to impose undue hardship on my mother. Back in the 1950s, that was the psychology of the times.

Even though Kim's passing left a glaring gap between the first four kids and the last four kids in my family, none of us appeared to be affected by it. Life went on. My mother spoke of it only when asked about it, and even then she did so in short, unemotional sentences.

We were known as a family of eight, but it would have been nine with Kim's presence. My standard refrain throughout my life was always, "I'm the seventh of eight kids." It was easier that way. Kim gradually became the nonexistent family member as though she had never been born at all. Years passed before I understood the depth of Mom's sorrow.

My first son was born at twenty-four weeks during the week of Christmas. Alone in my room and heavily sedated from the emergency C-section, I stared blindly out the window.

The phone rang. It was Mom, reaching out to me long-distance.

"You have a grandson, Mom," I announced brightly, masking my bleak spirits. "His name is Cody Travis."

"Oh, Jennifer, that's wonderful!" she answered with enthusiasm in an attempt to hide her concern. "How much does he weigh?"

"One pound, six ounces," I replied, my voice breaking.

"Oh, honey."

Her response, simple as it was, spoke volumes. I could lose this baby.

Neither one of us dared say it out loud. As my deepest fear bubbled to the surface, tears stung my eyes, and I began to tremble, aching for her steady presence and her compassion and warmth. Only my mother, my beautiful mother, whose baby had been buried overseas so long ago, would understand.

"I love you, Mom," I whispered.

"I love you, too, hon."

Two days later, my parents wore scrubs in the NICU, absorbing the impact of the tiniest grandchild they had ever welcomed into this world. Watching my mother as she tenderly cupped Cody's head, I wondered if she was thinking of her little girl. Perhaps she was envisioning a place like this, complete with aggressive technology, saving her daughter just as it had saved her grandson.

A few years ago, Mom received a necklace for Mother's Day that featured little boy and girl stick figures with birthstones. There we were, all eight of us birthstone brats, dangling from a long gold chain. She wore it with great pride. The manner in which her fingers lightly trailed over each child touched me in particular.

Over one recent holiday, I handed Mom a small white box. The card read: "Mom, I just wanted to fill the gap between the first four and the last four." Puzzled, she opened her gift. It was a girl stick figure with Kim's emerald birthstone.

"It's Kim, Mom. The baby you lost."

Her eyes were moist as we hugged each other tight.

"You are so thoughtful," she said softly.

Kim will gain her rightful place on Mom's necklace. Right there in the middle, between the first four and the last four, will be her daughter, thus completing the family.

These days I tell people I'm the eighth of nine children. I do this out of respect for my sister. I do this out of respect for my mother, whose pain is locked away. And for all mothers who mourn the loss of their babies, I do this for you, too.

Her name was Kim Lorraine. In the spring of 1956, my sister tiptoed out of this world just as quietly as she entered it, leaving small footprints on our hearts.

Jennifer Oliver

With Us in Spirit

I stopped at a Hallmark shop the other day to buy Mother's Day cards for my daughter and daughter-in-law. The card aisle was a long one; there were Mother's Day cards appropriate to send to everyone, from your cleaning lady to your best friend. The colors were soft and spring-like, fitting for the month of May. I moved up and down the aisle looking for cards that worked for Karen and Amy, and suddenly, without any warning, an ache started deep inside. It swelled and moved upward, hit my heart, and pushed a tear from my eye.

My hand reached out to a card that I knew she'd love. It was lavender and purple, her favorite colors. I read the verse and smiled. This was the one I'd buy her if I could only send it to her. I slipped it back in the rack, but picked it up and read it again, then replaced it. I really wanted to buy it for her, but she had passed away more than two years ago. I could buy the card, write a special note, sign it with love, then seal and stamp it, but where would I send it? Heaven had no post office. A curtain of sadness dropped down and covered me like a shroud.

I'm a mother and a grandmother of four, but I still miss

my mom. I miss our long talks. She had little formal education, but she possessed a marvelous instinct and insight into human behavior. I learned so much listening to her observations. I miss the stories she told about her childhood in a coal-mining town. She made me appreciate the differences in people's lives. I miss the wonderful pies and cakes she made. I miss her terrific sense of humor and hearty laughter. I miss her hugs.

But when I look around my home, I see her in many places. I see her warm smile in photos carefully arranged in several different rooms. I see her every time I sift through my recipe box and finger the many cards with her handwriting, all so precious now. I see her when I use my rolling pin, once hers, now mine. Whenever I use it, I am reminded of the day she taught me how to put just the right amount of pressure on a pie crust. I see her when I show visitors to our guest room, for the bed is covered with a quilt she had made by hand.

On Mother's Day, I will be with my daughter and her family at a Mother's Day brunch. To spend the day with a child I love and her husband and children will give me great pleasure. It wouldn't surprise me if we sense another presence that day, for my mother will be with us in spirit, spreading her love once more.

Nancy Julien Kopp

Just Another Sandwich

*In three words I can sum up everything I've
learned about life: it goes on.*

Robert Frost

It didn't seem like much at first. Just a sandwich. Just
another tuna sandwich among the thousands of tuna
sandwiches I had made over the years for my boys.

I got out the bread, the tuna, mayo, spoon, knife, listening to our old cat screech and purr as I opened up the can.
Then it hit me—this was the last one.

I know, I know. A lot of wise moms insist their kids
make their own doggone lunches, thereby instilling a host
of positive traits, including a good work ethic and all sorts
of other great lifetime skills and abilities a child will need
in the outside world to be a fine, productive member of
society. But I've been strangely selfish on this task. I have
always liked the idea of doing this one act out of love for
my kids. I want to make sure they're eating right, even
though I know they are fully capable of tossing the whole
lunch, bag and all, into the trash as they head for the
vending machines. I even used to make elaborate cartoons

on their napkins every day, such is the weirdness of this mom. I stopped, for the most part, doing the rest, but making just the sandwich was something I held on to.

You see, it was one mom-thing I could still do that harkened back to days when little boys clutched canvas lunch boxes and couldn't wait to see what treat or goofy cartoon lay inside. I can still see them running to class, shoes untied, grinning at friends, and disappearing through massive double doors.

As my two sons grew, there was less and less I was able to do for them. This was good. This was the way it should be. After all, it was my job to teach my boys how to not need me. It was the definition of bittersweet. But I stubbornly continued to make the sandwiches, except for a few interruptions in middle school when school lunches were in vogue and home lunches were, well, dorky.

It's right, says the voice inside. *Letting go is the way it's supposed to be.* My mind knows this. My mind gets it. My mind has wrapped itself all around this fact and all things having to do with this fact for a long time now. It's my heart that doesn't understand, and I don't know how to tell it, because every time I try, I feel it breaking just a little.

In my two sons, now fine young men, I see faint glimmers of those little boys, divinely enhanced by the hand of God and the dance of time. Deep, robust laughter replaces nighttime giggles heard over the intercom, and pictures of school dress-up day with little clowns or spacemen are replaced with tuxedos and a corsage for prom night.

The pride my husband and I have felt in watching them grow does not dissipate. T-ball, soccer, karate, track, guitar-drum-French horn solos, open house art galleries at school, holiday band concerts, award ceremonies, when little eyes read first words, the first step, first bike, first Rollerblades, first skateboard, first car. No, the pride and joy in who they are never evaporates or pales, it continues to grow and grow and grow.

Like I said, it was just a tuna sandwich. But in the middle of spooning tuna salad on bread it hit me. Hard. *This is the last lunch I will make as the mother of a schoolboy.*

Some might say that I'm being ridiculous and tell me to get over it, but that's not me. I intend to feel it all, just as I've felt every handmade Mother's Day card, every big and little hug, every time I heard the words, "I love you Mommy!" (now morphed into a quick "Love you, Mom," as a young man heads for his car), every single dandelion bouquet, every moment of every precious God-given gem of a day. I'll feel it all, and feel it deeply.

I held the sandwich, now safely ensconced in a plastic bag, and thought for a moment about drawing a silly cartoon on a napkin for old time's sake. I then sighed and stopped. *No.* Now was not the time to look back and try to retrieve something or wish for yesterday. Today was a day to get out his graduation cap, iron his gown, and get ready for the new adventures. I thanked God I didn't sell all the days of their youth for a paycheck. We scrimped, we didn't save much, but we had a hefty bank account filled with memories that only a close family can deposit.

When my youngest son walks forward to receive his diploma, my tears will be from joy, not regret. I will sit in the stands knowing I did my best and will savor every single precious memory of being there, holding them, and watching them grow. Not one single memory gets left behind when that tassel is turned and that cap is tossed high into the air. The memories live right along with me.

I held the sandwich for a moment and blinked hard as I stared at it there in the cellophane. *It's just a sandwich. It's just a stupid sandwich.* But in that moment I could feel one era coming to an end and a new one waiting breathlessly just before me, anxious to begin.

Wiping my eyes, I called to my son, "Time to get going, honey. Your lunch is on the counter." I picked up my purse, kissed my boy on the head, and we made our commute to school one last time.

Change roars in whether we want it to or not, and I wasn't ready for this particular train. But no choice was given, so the best I could do was board, knowing the journey has been an incredible ride—and as a mom, it never ends. But one thing I know for sure; this mom will never see a simple tuna sandwich in the same way ever again.

Lindy Batdorf

A Sequel of Sunrises

We must be willing to let go of the life we have planned, so as to have the life that is waiting for us.

E. M. Forster

When he moved out, he left everything behind. His drums, his bike, his bedroom set. The posters left hanging on the wall echoed a young boy, preparing to make his way in the world someday. And that he did. Burning the midnight oil studying for exams and writing term papers, he attained the goal he had set for himself. He joined the ranks of psychologists. He's happy doing what he is doing. And I know he's happy, but I still miss him.

When she left, she took everything with her but the sewing machine. "Let's make this the sewing room," she said. "And a study." I agreed. Her books spill over from wall to wall. Children's books. Textbooks. Masterpieces in English literature. Books with lesson plans for first and second grades. She's a teacher now and on her own. And I know she's happy, but I still miss her.

When I drive into "the big city" to have lunch with my

son, I never get over that empty feeling that grabs me when I see him walking up the street toward me. Dressed in a shirt and tie, smiling through blue-tinted sunglasses, I realize that he has grown up. But I ask myself over and over again, *When did all this happen? What is he doing in a big city like Los Angeles? When did he let go of my hand and run ahead?*

"But do you have enough food in your refrigerator?" I ask him over a vegetarian pizza. "Are you getting enough rest?" Twenty inquiring questions. Twenty "I'm okay, Mom" responses. I take a bite of my pizza and swallow hard. I tell myself, *Just take three steps backward. Let him enjoy his new world.*

My daughter echoes a lot of the teaching techniques I thought came naturally to me. At an age when I am about to retire from teaching, I proudly pass the torch to my daughter. Having recently moved into her own apartment, I asked her, "Do you have enough food in your refrigerator? Do you get enough rest?" The voice inside me says, *Let her enjoy her independence. You enjoyed yours.*

Mornings are hardest for me. When I open my bedroom shades and look out onto the back driveway, I notice that both cars are gone. The spaces my son and daughter used to park in are empty. A million thoughts race through my mind as I make my way to the kitchen and my morning coffee. *How can I keep the world from hurting my children now that they are "out there"? What if they need me in the middle of the night, and I'm not around to help them?* Then the voice inside me makes me realize they are not little children anymore. *But what does that voice know anyway?* I ask myself. *Is it a mother?*

I wonder if my mother had these lost feelings when I left home. She helped me plan my wedding, made sure I had everything I needed to start a life away from home, and waved good-bye as I drove down the street. When she put her hand to her face, was she crying?

My mom will soon turn ninety-one. And she still worries about me. And I worry about her. I believe motherhood is a forever thing, and I wouldn't have it any other way. Being a mother has enriched my life because I have shared it with my children. And I hope I have enriched my mother's life. I guess that's what it's all about. The circle of life.

Maybe my mom *was* crying on the day I drove down the street after my wedding. And maybe I cry after I leave the restaurant, having had lunch with my son. And maybe I cry after I visit my daughter's classroom as a visiting teacher. But crying is allowed. And so is worrying about if they have enough food in their refrigerators and if they get enough rest. I'm concerned about their well-being, because they are my children, and I am their mother. And I wish them a good life.

Lola De Julio De Maci

And He Flew

Wheresoever you go, go with all your heart.

Confucius

"It's a gorgeous day for it, Mom. There's not a cloud in the sky! It's a little hazy, but that should burn off in an hour or so." Tim was excited, and that was understandable. After all, he had been working toward this for almost three years; he had saved his money and sacrificed his free time. He spent every spare minute working at the airport, washing and cleaning airplanes.

We paid for the instructor, and he paid for the plane rental—that was the deal. He held up his end of the bargain and now, at the tender age of sixteen, he was about to solo. He had been dreaming of this day since he was three years old, and now it was here. One long cross-country solo flight, and a check ride, were all that stood between Tim and a private pilot's license. All the study time, all the long hours, all the uncertainty and fear must have dissipated somewhere along the way. Here he was today, huddled with his instructor, getting some last minute advice.

A few minutes later, he ran over to the car where I was

waiting. (I had to drive him here since he did not yet have a driver's license.) We had been through this routine several times over the past few months, and it always ended the same way. We'd drive to the airport, he'd get into the plane, go through his checklist, and prepare for his solo flight, only to find it was canceled due to wind, fog, haze, or any number of meteorological anomalies. I was always secretly relieved, yet part of me felt sad for him because he was so disappointed. This weekly drill had become quite comfortable, and I only half listened to his chatter about the weather and the possibility of yet another cancellation. Still, my thoughts were distracted by the small, bright rays of sun peeking through the early morning fog; somehow I knew that today would be the day. My son was enthusiastic as he ran into the airport to call the weather service, and I sat in the car, almost completely consumed by fear. Finally, I shouted to myself, "Stop it!" I quickly looked around to see if anyone had heard me, but everything seemed to be normal.

People were going about their business, and no one appeared to take notice of me at all. I was becoming increasingly nervous and anxious. *Movement, that's what I needed,* I thought. I walked around the hangar and chastised myself on the way back to the car, vowing to pull myself together. "After all," I said, "he's a bright, intelligent, capable young man. And according to his flight instructor, 'He has a natural gift—he was born to fly.'" I liked the sound of those words, and my head knew that they were probably true.

But my heart responded, *He's only sixteen! He lacks the experience and wisdom that accompanies age.* I suddenly remembered when watching *Sesame Street* was the most important part of his day, and how he insisted on wearing his Bert and Ernie bedroom slippers while he watched the show. Now this! When did it all happen, this growing up thing? And why wasn't I prepared for it? I had spent the last sixteen years nurturing, guiding, teaching, and loving him more than any living thing on earth. He had learned to be confident, self-assured, and independent. He had discovered how to live his life without my protection, and he was doing it now, right in front of me! I had done a good job preparing him to take risks and to face life's challenges, and he was doing that admirably.

Suddenly, I found my fear returning as I looked up just in time to watch the fog lift, revealing the bluest sky I had ever seen. Against the background of that clear, blue sky, I watched my only son run to the car and announce to me with great joy that he was going to complete his long solo flight, at last. "And, Mom," Tim said jokingly, "Please don't take a picture of me beside the plane this time. It's embarrassing." I agreed and sat on a bench watching from a distance as he prepared the plane and himself for the journey. It seemed to take forever; he checked everything. When he was satisfied, he flashed me a thumbs-up signal, climbed into the cockpit alone, and closed the door. At that moment I was paralyzed by panic. The sight and sound of the door closing behind him made it all so final, and a thousand terrifying thoughts spun simultaneously through my head. *What if the engine quits? What if he gets sick? What if he faints? What if he gets lost or runs out of fuel or has a midair collision with a jumbo jet?* By now I was sobbing and drawing a crowd. Better to pray and wait at home than to stay and make a scene, so I left.

A couple of hours later, the phone rang. Tim had made it safely one way, and now only the return trip remained. I hurried back to the airport where I waited and prayed even harder, much more composed and strangely convinced that he would return safely.

Again, my thoughts drifted to a helpless little boy who had somehow grown into a courageous young man. He would never be the same after this experience, nor would I. Just then, my musings were interrupted by the sound of a plane high overhead—it was Tim. He had made it home! As I watched his flawless landing, I thought how raising a child was like being a mother bird nestled high among the cliffs. Each day the baby birds come a few steps closer to the brink, then one day, with the greatest reluctance, the mother bird gently pushes them off the edge of the cliff—and they fly!

Today, my "baby" flew. Unlike the mother bird, I didn't push. Instead, he jumped.

Ellen L. Boyd

8

THANK YOU, MOM

A mother is a person, who, seeing there are only four pieces of pie for five people, promptly announces she never did care for pie.

Tenneva Jordan

Flowers for Mother

We can let circumstances rule us, or we can take charge and rule our lives from within.

Earl Nightingale

When time flies backward in my memory, I find myself standing in front of a lilac bush. I am eight years old, and it is Mother's Day. But it's the Depression years, money is scarce, and I have nothing to give my mother. I take out the scissors I found in Mother's sewing basket and snip the prettiest lilac. Laying it in a shoebox, I tie it with a string and creep upstairs to Mother's bedroom. Ever so quietly, I place my treasure at Mother's door, and just as silently, I make my way back downstairs.

Fast-forward forty-six years. Cleaning out Mother's things after her death at eighty-one, I found the old shoebox with the dried lilac still inside. Also inside was the love of a little girl, as fresh as ever. Mother was a single parent during the early part of the century when, unlike today, it wasn't accepted as part of "the norm." She found employment at a downtown department store and rode the streetcar to and from work. She was as thrilled to see me waiting for her at the car stop as I was to see her step off the streetcar. She always had a small treat for me, a stick of gum, a bit of candy, or a funny postcard. With arms around each other, we walked the two blocks home.

As much as Mother worked hard to be both a mother and a dad, I remember sitting on the front porch watching the fathers of my friends come home at night. I envied the way they were greeted, just like heroes coming home from a long war. I wanted someone who I could call "Dad," someone who would greet me like that. At times I felt guilty for feeling that way, because I knew Mother worked hard to provide for me the best she could.

I remember the day of my twelfth birthday. Mother had invited four little girls to our house for cake and ice cream. After we played games, Mother called me to the front yard. Pulling up to the curb was a big truck, and we watched as the driver opened the doors in the back and pulled out a brand new bicycle! I had never seen anything so beautiful—it was red and white with green stripes. No one in the neighborhood had a beauty like that, and I couldn't believe it was mine. I asked Mother many years later how she could have afforded such a gift, and she said she had to sign a note to pay one dollar a week for eight months.

When summertime came, Mother scraped enough together for a season swim ticket at Crystal Pool, and as I grew into my teens, I never felt left out of any events because I couldn't afford a ticket or a fare. When my junior high school put on their operetta, I was selected as one of the main cast and needed a different gown for the two nights it was performed. I was afraid to tell Mother about the gowns, because I knew how expensive they could be, but Mother scoured the shops and found two beautiful dresses on sale—one white and one pink—and again she said she had to pay each week on credit. During the curtain call on the second night of the performance, I was handed a beautiful bouquet of flowers; it was a gift from my mother.

The years passed, and when I was married during World War II, Mother rode the bus with me out to Nebraska for my Army chapel wedding. I didn't have a dad to walk me down the chapel aisle, but Mother proudly provided that part of the service. She was present when each of our five children was born and was as great a grandmother as she was a mother.

When Mother was hospitalized for a biopsy, she was asked by the nurse if she had anything valuable she wanted to put into safe keeping. Her answer: "Yes, my daughter." She passed away two weeks later, and I've missed her for the past thirty years. She was my role model, my protector, my mentor, and my best friend. It was an honor to be able to share her love and devotion with others.

Mary Emily Dess

The Evolution

My mother and I had reached that point in our relationship where we became friends, and then I had a stroke and everything changed. Before the stroke, I had just come to the realization she was human and therefore imperfect, and that was okay. She, in turn, became acquainted with a young, independent woman who shared her love for reading, doing crafts, playing games, and remodeling old houses.

I remember sitting in her living room, our heads bent over our embroidery while I taught her needlepoint stitches. She shared her knowledge of painting ceramics and drawing. Whether it was frequenting garage sales, gambling, traveling, or just spending the day on the porch in silent revelry, we enjoyed spending time together.

She was my dear friend. No longer was she obligated to discipline me. Now we could be who we were, two women with commonalities and differences who respected and genuinely liked each other.

My stroke transported us back to an earlier time. She was forced back into her role of mother, because I returned to my role of child. I refused to take an active part in decision making with regard to my life. Even the clothes I wore were selected by my mother, because I refused to make even the most rudimentary decisions. I hid in sleep and wallowed in my depression. And I felt that, at twenty-six, my life was over. I was a ventilator-dependent quadriplegic with no hope or faith. I wanted to die, but my mom wouldn't allow it. She had the strength and faith to wait for better days.

Each day she moved my unfeeling limbs, hoping my brain would reconnect with my body. She demanded I watch while she put my fingers through the range of motion exercises. "Try to move your finger," she insisted doggedly. I tried, and when I succeeded, her determination to see me restored consumed her days. From morning till night, she attempted to move every joint, with her patient mother's determination. Function returned in my left arm and hand, and I could turn my head and wiggle my toes.

These milestones fueled her dreams of a daughter with a happy future. I was only cooperative because, when I was, she would be happy and leave me alone. Sleep was my hiding place, and I gratefully sank into its numbing embrace every chance I got. I was an unwilling participant in life, but my mother had enough drive for both of us.

Energized by her successes, she prodded my diaphragm dozens of times a day and asked, "Do you feel this? Can you feel this?" For three months she tirelessly performed this ritual, and I responded like a petulant child.

"No, Mother, I can't," I answered with a look full of resentment. I wondered what it would take for her to give up.

One day my answer differed. "I'm not sure. Do it again." She did, and I felt it. I thought, *Now maybe she'll stop.* But I was wrong; my answer had heralded the beginning of her crusade. My mother was going to get me to breathe unassisted by the ventilator.

Days stretched into weeks, weeks into months, and months into years. I tired of her relentless pursuit of reawakening my body. Like a teenager growing into adulthood, I bucked against the constraints of my mother's influence. Once again, I tried to exert my independence, and did not stop to thank her for the time and dedication she had given me. All I saw was that the eight hours of therapy a day became intolerable. "Mom, I would rather not get any movement or sensation back, because all I do is dream of what might be. I want a life again. I'm going to live with what I've got."

Mom struggled against her mother's instincts to push me further. It was not in her nature to give up when there was the possibility of restoring more of my movement. I was no longer compliant to her demands. After she had devoted herself to the thankless task of rehabilitating my body, I began to focus on my spirit. She had to loosen her bonds and allow me to exert my will and fulfill my desires. At times I made wrong decisions, and she watched me fail and helped me pick up the pieces of my wounded psyche.

Today we have come almost full circle. She is still devoted to me and steps into her role of mother when I need her. Day to day we are friends. I can no longer stitch embroidery or physically remodel a house, but we recently bought a house and are planning the renovation together. I would not be where I am today if she had not fought for me when I wouldn't fight for myself, or if she had refused to let me exert my independence again. I thank her for today and all of my tomorrows, because without her I never would have become me—a writer, a speaker, and more than just her daughter—a friend, once again.

Jessica Kennedy

On Being a Mother

Nothing is so strong as gentleness and nothing is so gentle as real strength.

Ralph W. Sockman

I have a picture of my mother-in-law that I just love. At one of our girls' birthday parties, the camera caught Mother Hart in a moment of pure joy, laughter lighting up her face. I choose to think of her this way.

It was not always so. As a much younger woman, still on the slopes of Fool's Hill myself, I was jealous of her ability to command my husband's attention with a word. I worried that he loved her more than me. On the other hand, Mother Hart wondered if I could or would make her son happy or be a good mother to her grandchildren. She worried that her son would leave her forever. She might have been a little jealous of me.

As time went by, we established a truce. I needed to remind myself often that she had done at least one thing right—she raised my husband to be a loving, caring, honest man. She had to remember that she did not get to pick her son's wife, and that she really just wanted her son to be happy.

Mother Hart and I edged closer and closer over the years, never really sure of one another, but willing to try because of the things we held in common. And then my own mother died.

Mama and I had our ups and downs over the years, but we had as close a relationship as people who lived two thousand miles apart could. When Mama got sick, my husband and I brought her to Texas to live with us. Mother Hart knew Mama was dying, and she planned to visit once Mama got settled in. She wanted to meet my mother.

That was not to be. Mama died three weeks after I brought her home. My husband called to tell her; that conversation changed our relationship forever. I sat listening to them on the phone, not really able to talk, but when Mother Hart asked, "Do you want me to come?" I managed to blurt out "Yes, please."

Mother Hart helped me through the most painful time of my life. She dropped her own life and came to take care of me. In doing so, she showed me my importance in her life. She did not say or do anything magical; she just showed up, and her presence was a gift. She took care of the mundane chores, washing dishes and such, but what mattered most was the connection she gave me.

Something happens when your mother dies. If she outlived your father, or if your relationship was close, you can feel like the world has cast you adrift, like you have no one to turn to. In some ways, I have never felt more truly alone than when my mother died, but Mother Hart's being there helped. She never tried to step into Mama's place. She simply let me know that I still had a family—her family.

I learned a lot from those few days Mother Hart spent with us. I learned that she really did love me, that our days of mutual toleration had ended. She showed me that I am not, and will never have to be, alone. I realized I had proven myself to her over the years, and she had fully accepted my place in her son's life and her own. I also recognized that she had a place in my life and that she was no threat to me. I have realized since then that the love between us was planted, tended, and grown, rather than just appearing. This kind of love is perfectly acceptable, perhaps even preferable to the volunteer variety, since one thinks twice before trampling on a carefully cultivated relationship.

On the slopes of Fool's Hill, vision is distorted. Youth and inexperience color every perception. A man's mother cannot make or unmake his marriage, if it is built on a solid foundation, even if it looks like she can. And no girl can destroy a man's love for his mother. She merely takes a place his mother can never fill.

People die, and when they do, we lose them forever, except in memory. I try to be more careful than ever to make memories we all want to keep. I cannot know if Mother Hart will ever need me the way I needed her, but I plan to be there if she does.

Ann Weaver Hart

A Journey to Remember

Some painters transform the sun into a yellow spot, others transform a yellow spot into the sun.

Pablo Picasso

My mailbox was filled with requests for money and advertisements for children's tiger T-shirts. My impending tenth college reunion at Princeton was coming up, and these pleas for my wallet were getting more intense.

However, one notice stood out. John Wilmerding, my thesis professor in the art and archaeology department, was retiring. As I opened the envelope, I drifted back to those mesmerizing works of Early American art that illuminated the darkened classrooms. Wilmerding demanded intellectual curiosity and rigor, but tempered that exigency with his humor and wit. While Wilmerding has certainly left a brilliant legacy—his leadership at the National Gallery of Art, numerous publications, and donated works of art—his greatest legacy cannot be easily summed up on a résumé. Exceptional teachers affect more than just their students. Their magnetism reaches beyond the classroom, and Wilmerding unwittingly enriched a bond between a dying mother and her daughter through his teaching.

My mother was a little bit nuts, lovable, but a bit nuts. She only lived an hour and a half away from Princeton and took that fact as an open invitation to come for a visit any time she pleased. She would show up in my college dorm at 6:00 AM on Sundays with bags of groceries and fresh donuts. While my roommates enjoyed the fresh strawberries and chocolate fritters, they did not appreciate the early morning wake-up calls.

Whisking my mother over a passed-out roommate, we would trot by the nighttime revelers scuffling their way back home to be the first ones on line at PJ's Pancake House. It was there that she was first introduced to John Wilmerding—not in person at first, but vicariously. While munching on chocolate-chip pancake stacks, I would share the details of that week's mesmerizing lecture of Early American art. Although my most difficult, his class was my favorite. Weaving the background stories of the artists with the moments captured on canvas, Professor Wilmerding would unravel the mysteries of the image to us. Like a compelling detective story, we would be introduced to all of the facts—an examined look at the brushstrokes, research into the artist's dreams, the placement of the objects—and watch as the clues became untangled. I was always disappointed when class came to an end. The lights would turn on, abruptly closing the pages on those absorbing stories until the next lecture.

My mother soaked in these magical stories. She was captivated. I was captivated. It only took a few more breakfast dates (although many calories later), before she played hooky from work to attend Professor Wilmerding's lectures in person. The door would open just a crack a few minutes after the lecture had begun and a figure would quickly enter the darkened room. While she would always sit in the back row, she was obviously the most engrossed one in the classroom. A perennial student, she fit right in (sort of).

Those classroom visits to Professor Wilmerding's lectures ended abruptly my senior year. At the beginning of the school year, she was diagnosed with stage 4 ovarian cancer and had only a few more months to live. A true bibliophile, she was able to lose the pain within the pages of her books and find solace in the character's triumphs. However, once morphine was prescribed, the words became just as cluttered as the disease. I knew how desperately she wished to hide in the back of the cozy slide rooms of McCormick Hall and take copious notes on the secrets and stories that Wilmerding would unveil. Cancer now enveloped her, not those dark lights and beautiful images.

Looking back now, what I did was probably against campus policy, but I snuck a mini audio recorder into Professor Wilmerding's lectures in an attempt to capture his words so that I could bring at least a piece of these magical college moments back to her sterile hospital room. However, I could not afford a very expensive recorder, and what turned out on the tape was nothing more than a mumbled mess.

Not one to give up, I brought my art history notebook along with me and tried to re-create the thrill of Professor Wilmerding's lectures for her, which she enjoyed. She passed away later that fall, but she took with her the adventure through art that John Wilmerding created in each lecture. And what a magnificent journey it was to share with her.

Michelle Gannon

Handful of Love

"It's going to be Mother's Day soon," I was reminded by my five-year-old son, Cody. My thoughts immediately turned to what we could give my mother and mother-in-law, and when would I find the time to go and get it, working full-time and juggling the schedules of three children. Of course, I didn't have to worry about what my kids were getting for me, for Mother's Day was the one special day when their daddy was in charge of the gift buying.

Cody, of course, didn't have to wait for the sacred trip to the Big K or Wal-Mart with Dad. "I made you something for Mother's Day at school, and it's beautiful," Cody continued. "Do you want to know what it is?" I assured him that while I couldn't wait to see it, I also loved surprises, and maybe he should try and keep it a secret just a few more days. Having had similar conversations with my daughter, Ashley, now fourteen, and other son, Micheal, eleven, I knew this would be pretty tough for my kindergartener.

For the next four days, I got updates on my present on the way home from the babysitter's place. "The paint's almost dry," and "I picked pretty colors for you, Mama," and "I had to wrap it real careful because it's 'fragible.'"

Cody could hardly contain his excitement, and I could hardly wait to see it myself!

Finally, Mother's Day arrived. From my husband, I received one of those mushy, "I-still-adore-you" cards. From Ashley and Micheal, I received hanging flower baskets that looked lovely on our front porch, along with a quirky little card reminding me how boring my life would be without them, not that I needed reminding!

Then it was time for Cody's gift, which was carefully wrapped in a bright pink package. And what did I receive from Cody? What almost every child has given their Mama at one time or another—a plaster of Paris print of his little hand, painted in an array of lovely colors. I felt the sting of tears behind my eyes, knowing that this would probably be the last little handprint I would be blessed to receive. It was not only the handprint itself, which was precious, but also the love, hard work, and pride found in a small child's heart to show his Mama how much she is loved.

Debra C. Butler

Moms Cry

In the corner of my dresser drawer is a small, folded pink dress. It has pearl buttons, a lace collar, and a silky, pink ribbon sash that goes around the middle. It has not always been in my drawer, however.

Before my mom went to heaven, this same dress remained in her dresser drawer for twenty-eight years. Now when I look at it, my eyes overflow with tears of joy, as it is a reminder of the love and comfort God gave me through my mom, Betty.

I was adopted when I was six years old. For quite a while, I could not comprehend that I really had a mom. I called out "Betty" when I needed another spoon to dig in the sandbox. I called out "Betty" when I needed a drink of Kool-Aid. One night I had awakened from a bad dream, and it was "Betty" who heard me crying and came to chase the monsters away. One day I fell; my knee was bleeding, and I was scared. "Betty" was there to comfort me and make it all better. And as she placed a yellow Band-Aid on my knee and kissed away the hurt, for the first time I simply looked up at her, smiled, and said, "Thank you, Mom." And for the first time, I saw my mom cry.

Growing up, life's wounds sometimes needed bigger

Band-Aids. When that happened, Mom was always there. As a teen, I began to question who I was and where I had come from. Mom didn't always have the answers to my questions, but when she didn't, she would take me to her bedroom and, once again, show me the neatly folded pink dress that was in her dresser drawer.

I had seen the dress numerous times. Mom would point out the pearl buttons, the lace collar, and the pink sash that tied around the middle. And once again, through her tears, she would tell me, "This is the dress you wore the day you became my daughter." And in sharing that special moment with me, she comforted me.

I still remember wearing the little pink dress, twirling around and making swishy noises with the ruffled petticoat underneath. At those moments I truly felt like a fairy princess. Also, in that moment of remembering, the answers to my questions seemed less important. I simply knew I was a princess, because I had a mom named Betty, and I was loved.

This is why moms cry, I've learned. God gives them tears to express the outpouring of love their hearts cannot express in words. Does anything else really matter?

Nancy Barnes

Cancer's Gift

Just living is not enough. One must have sun-shine, freedom, and a little flower.

Hans Christian Andersen

When I was forty-three years old, I was diagnosed with breast cancer. My doctor recommended several rounds of chemotherapy. After taking chemotherapy for five days in a row, it was very difficult for me to fall asleep at night. This phenomenon has been explained as a type of drug withdrawal. Exhausted, I would lie in my bed for hours, unable to sleep.

Enter my mother—five foot nothing with curly brown hair and huge blue eyes. She was in her seventies and in extremely poor health. Among her ailments, osteoporosis had caused her back to become very humped. This made it uncomfortable for her to stand for long periods of time. But stand she did. On those nights when I was unable to sleep, she would stand at my bedside for hours rubbing my back, sometimes as late as 4:00 AM. While she rubbed, she shared stories of her sister and mother who had died before I was born. I learned much about her childhood and her days as a young woman.

Ignoring the pain in her back, my mother kept rubbing mine until she was sure I was asleep. More than once I lay quiet and still, slowing my breathing on purpose. She would softly whisper my name, and finally assured that I was sleeping, she would shuffle off to bed.

Cancer is a horrible, frightening disease. But sometimes wonderful gifts come out of the darkest times in our lives. One of my most special memories will always be of my little mother standing beside my bed rubbing my back when she had need of someone to rub hers. It was the gift of a mother's sacrificial love.

Verna Wood

Everything Is Possible

Life consists not in holding good cards but in playing those you hold well.

Josh Billings

Everything is possible. How many times had my mother told me that? She could say that. She had never tried to get a hit off Mongo, that fire-balling lefthander from Morristown, or attempted to get a perfect score on one of Mrs. Bach's spelling tests. Mrs. Bach always put in a couple of tricky words that were actually spelled the way they sounded.

We were sitting on the front steps of our old farmhouse one warm summer night. This was something my mother and I did a lot when the mosquitoes would allow it. We had no air conditioning, so it was a little cooler on the steps, and I guess we just sat there waiting for my father to build us a front porch—a place where we could sit and watch the world go by. Dad never did get around to that, as he was too busy milking cows. The steps were a great place to talk. We would listen to the birds getting in their final songs before darkness fell. We would listen to the frogs and toads romancing their mates. This particular night, we watched a large airplane fly overhead. We wondered where the occupants were headed while we sat on our steps.

"I sure would like to fly in one of those things someday," I said.

"Everything is possible," my mother replied.

Ha! A lot she knew about it. Neither my mother nor my father had ever set foot on a plane, let alone flown in one. It was then that I saw the fireflies blinking along the edges of our yard. The flashes of the lightning bugs demanded that they be watched.

"Get the jar!" ordered my mother enthusiastically.

I got the large jar from my upstairs bedroom. It was a jar meant for collecting and holding insects. It was equipped with a lid with air holes poked into it in order to make the fireflies' short stay as comfortable as possible. We would normally observe captives for only a brief time before releasing them unharmed. I presented the jar to my mother for her approval.

"Let's catch some fireflies!" she said.

We chased and we caught. My mother was much better at chasing than she was at catching. We laughed a lot. The fireflies may have done some laughing, too. Who knows? After a bit, I had caught a number of the elusive fireflies. I placed the jar near the steps where we sat. The jar glowed in the night. Mom and I smiled. We watched in silence until another airplane flew over, its lights blinking across the dark sky.

"Yup," I said, "I'd sure like to fly in an airplane one day."

"Everything is possible," my mother said once more.

"Do you really think that's so?" I asked as I picked up the jar and prepared to release its luminescent prisoners.

"How can someone holding a jar full of stars believe that anything is impossible?" asked my mother.

I have managed to fly on a number of airplanes, but I still chase fireflies.

Al Batt

Love and Forgiveness

To err is human; to forgive, divine.

Alexander Pope

I had only been home from the hospital with my new-born daughter a couple of days when my husband suggested I give my aunt a call. To anyone else, that request would seem perfectly normal. In this situation, however, it had a special meaning. I was adopted, and she was my birth mother. And she didn't know that I knew.

Growing up as an only child, I had devoted parents. We were a close-knit family, and I never questioned their love, even when, at ten years old, I found out I was adopted. The rumor had come through some neighborhood kids from the daughter of a friend of my mom's. My mother was devastated that she didn't tell me first, but it meant nothing to me. So secure was I in my parents' love that this revelation was completely irrelevant to my life. Yet even at that young age, I sensed how deeply it upset her. For some reason, she was sure this knowledge would change my feelings for them. Nothing I said persuaded her otherwise. So I tucked that understanding away in my heart, stopped talking about it, and continued to enjoy growing up.

As I became a teenager, I grew curious about my heritage. Who did I look like? Where did they come from? Did I have any siblings? These questions sent my imagination into overdrive and convinced me to investigate. So one day when my parents were gone, I looked through my dad's files and found my adoption papers. That's when I discovered the truth about my aunt. It was her name on the line for consenting mother.

I was, of course, absolutely stunned. For a little while I just sat there staring at the paper, unable to thoroughly grasp what this meant. Then slowly it became evident that this was a profound secret. Nothing had ever happened to raise my suspicions or cause me to even consider that I was adopted inside my family. More important, if my mother had been so concerned that I knew I was adopted, how would she feel if she knew what I had discovered? She and I had such an amazing relationship, and I loved her dearly—there was absolutely no way I was going to take a chance of hurting her with this. So I folded the paper, put it away, and determined never, ever to let her know I knew. And I never did. Our relationship remained strong and wonderful until the sad day she died eight years later from a cancerous brain tumor.

Now, two years after her death, I sat thinking about my husband's suggestion. Maybe this was the right thing to do, to get the secret out. But I was terrified. I had never known my "aunt" very well because she had always lived in another state. She was always cordial, and I liked her. Yet, once the truth was out, would my "aunt" expect me to feel something for her that I didn't? She might have given me life, but she wasn't my mother. My mother was the person who had held me when I was sick, taught me to cook, encouraged me at every turn, and helped me through those emotional preteen and teenage years. I loved her so much. She was the one who I missed more than ever as I looked in the face of the grandchild she would never know. Yet, could this grandchild be the very reason the secret should come out? What would I tell my little girl about my being adopted? With those questions in my mind, I decided to make the call. I didn't know what would happen, but I knew it was time to tell the truth.

When my aunt answered the phone, she was very surprised to hear from me, but she was kind, and it eased my anxiety. Then, after telling her about my daughter, I told her what I knew. She was quiet, shocked with my confession. Her first question was, "How did you find out?" I related finding the adoption papers, but explained that I never shared my discovery with my mom. Then I waited. It was apparent this was something she had never expected. I'm not sure now how I thought she would react, but her response was something I will never forget.

"You had a mom," she said, "and it wasn't me. I gave you birth, but I couldn't take care of you. So I gave you to my sister, and she loved you. You are the woman you are because of her, not because of me. I promised her the day she took you home that I would never cause a problem and never tell you that you were really mine. And I had committed to keep that promise to her even though she is no longer here. She did something for me that I couldn't do; she raised you, and I will always be grateful to her for that. I know that you loved your mom, and I don't expect you to love me that way. But I hope that we can have a relationship in the future, because I do love you, too."

I could hardly speak as the tears rolled down my face. It was such a relief to know that she didn't expect me to love her like I loved my mom, and she had allowed me to have a normal life by unselfishly keeping her promise. I was so glad to know how she felt and to understand how deeply she had cared about me and my mom. It certainly eased my mind, and the doubts about my decision to call immediately faded. A month after we spoke, she came for a visit. It was a good beginning to our relationship, and she shared everything I didn't know about the situation surrounding my birth. I realized even more the sacrifice she had made by giving me up.

Soon after that, I had another daughter, and many years later, I am now a grandmother. I've come to appreciate beyond words the relationship I have with my birth mother. We share memories and stories, and she's been the grandmother to my girls that my mom couldn't be. I'm thankful I didn't allow unfounded fear to rob me of someone who means the world to me now. Yes, I had a wonderful mother, and now I'm fortunate to have my birth mother. We share an amazing bond for which I will forever be thankful.

Kim Johnson

Her Greatest Achievement

Most human beings have an almost infinite capacity for taking things for granted.

Aldous Huxley

I'll never forget the day I asked her the question, nor will I ever forget her answer. I had nearly finished my senior year of high school. I had chosen my college, received an academic scholarship, and was hard at work trying to decide between a career as a foreign diplomat or a famous journalist for the *New York Times*.

She was where she usually was at the end of each weekday, in the kitchen making dinner. She wore a colorful cotton apron over her working clothes, and she had exchanged her high heels for comfortable house slippers.

She hummed to herself as she made meatloaf and peeled potatoes. Sandy, my six-year-old sister, sat by the window, coloring her third picture of a house, complete with chimney and a smiling sun in the corner of the page.

I busied myself with setting the table. I was impatient, as I often was in those days, to get on with my life and escape the humdrum domesticity of school and home. I had great dreams of accomplishing all sorts of things once I left home.

"What makes life worthwhile for you, Mother? What do you think has been your greatest achievement?" I blurted out of the blue.

I don't know if she heard the judgment behind the words, that her life was worth very little, that she spent her days working for a local company as a bookkeeper and her nights keeping up with the myriad tasks of a mother, wife, and homemaker. More so, my words made it sound that none of it counted for much, although I knew that even with my scholarship, her working hard every day would help to make up the difference, so I could attend the expensive school I had chosen.

She answered without hesitation. "Giving birth to you and your sister, loving and raising the two of you—that's my greatest achievement."

How I pitied her! I knew I would go so much further in life. I'd be a great writer or diplomat or I'd discover something of vital importance to all of humanity. If I had children at all, they certainly wouldn't take up so much of my life that they'd be my greatest achievement. What good would that do?

The next fall, I went to college. Eventually I went to law school, had my own law practice, and created several other interesting careers as years went by. I got married and had two children, just like her. Best of all, I discovered something of vital importance to all of humanity: that parenting requires the very best of ourselves. Being a mother taught me virtually all I needed to know about being a person of worth and character.

If someone asks me today what my greatest achievement in life has been, I'll give the same answer she did, so many years ago. And then I'll tell them who gave me such a wise answer.

Maril Crabtree

"Every day is Mother's Day around here."

More Chicken Soup?

Many of the stories and poems you have read in this book were submitted by readers like you who had read earlier Chicken Soup for the Soul books. We publish many Chicken Soup for the Soul books every year. We invite you to contribute a story to one of these future volumes.

Stories may be up to twelve hundred words and must uplift or inspire. You may submit an original piece, something you have read, or your favorite quotation on your refrigerator door.

To obtain a copy of our submission guidelines and a listing of upcoming Chicken Soup books, please write, fax, or check our website.

Please send your submissions to:

Chicken Soup for the Soul
Website: www.chickensoup.com
P.O. Box 30880
Santa Barbara, CA 93130
Fax: 805-563-2945

We will be sure that both you and the author are credited for your submission.

For information about speaking engagements, other books, audiotapes, workshops, and training programs, please contact any of our authors directly.

Supporting Others

With each Chicken Soup for the Soul book published, a charity is designated to receive a portion of the proceeds. A portion of the proceeds from this book will be donated to Project Cuddle.

Project Cuddle is the result of one woman's crusade to help prevent infants from being abandoned. Debbe Magnusen fostered over thirty drug-exposed babies, while raising two biological children. Eventually five of those beautiful little ones were adopted and became part of the Magnusen family.

Project Cuddle's crisis line was initially launched from the living room of Debbe's home, with the hope of ending baby abandonment. Within twelve hours of opening the twenty-four-hour crisis line, Project Cuddle got its first crisis call. A frightened woman who had hidden her pregnancy from everyone she knew was due to deliver and had had no prenatal care. There was no time to waste. Debbe had only days to orchestrate a safe and legal alternative to abandonment. Project Cuddle was able to retain an attorney, a family wanting to rescue and adopt the baby, as well as an obstetrician, hospital, and social counselor. Debbe Magnusen coached this woman through the delivery of a beautiful baby girl. After the baby was placed in the arms of the adoptive parents, the birth mother said to Debbe, "I feel like I've done something good for the first time." The woman did not break the law, the baby was safe, and a rescue couple was overjoyed at having a new daughter in their lives.

Tragically, babies are being abandoned across the nation on a daily basis. Since its inception, Project Cuddle has saved over 600 babies in the United States and Canada from the fate of being abandoned, or worse. John Stamos is the national spokesperson for the organization. With John's help, the charity has been able to create a school video to educate students on the importance of calling for help instead of abandoning a baby. Oprah and John recently surprised Debbe by featuring Project Cuddle on *The Oprah Winfrey Show*.

Project Cuddle was incorporated as a 501(c)(3) non-profit charity in 1994. A volunteer board of directors oversees the organization, which Debbe runs on a day-to-day basis with the assistance of volunteers and a minimally paid staff. Your generous donations are always appreciated and help to save the lives of more babies from the fate of abandonment.

To learn more, please contact Project Cuddle at:

Project Cuddle
2973 Harbor Boulevard, #326
Costa Mesa, CA 92626
Toll free: 888-628-3353
Phone: 714-432-9681
Website: www.projectcuddle.org

Who Is Jack Canfield?

Jack Canfield is the cocreator and editor of the Chicken Soup for the Soul series, which *Time* magazine has called "the publishing phenomenon of the decade." The series now has 105 titles with over 100 million copies in print in forty-one languages. Jack is also the coauthor of eight other bestselling books, including *The Success Principles: How to Get from Where You Are to Where You Want to Be; Dare to Win; The Aladdin Factor; You've Got to Read This Book;* and *The Power of Focus: How to Hit Your Business and Personal and Financial Targets with Absolute Certainty.*

Jack has recently developed a telephone coaching program and an online coaching program based on his most recent book, *The Success Principles.* He also offers a seven-day Breakthrough to Success seminar every summer, which attracts 400 people from fifteen countries around the world.

Jack has conducted intensive personal and professional development seminars on the principles of success for over 900,000 people in twenty-one countries around the world. He has spoken to hundreds of thousands of others at numerous conferences and conventions and has been seen by millions of viewers on national television shows such as *The Today Show, Fox and Friends, Inside Edition, Hard Copy,* CNN's *Talk Back Live, 20/20, Eye to Eye,* the *NBC Nightly News,* and the *CBS Evening News.*

Jack is the recipient of many awards and honors, including three honorary doctorates and a Guinness World Records Certificate for having seven books from the Chicken Soup for the Soul series appearing on the *New York Times* bestseller list on May 24, 1998.

To write to Jack or for inquiries about Jack as a speaker, his coaching programs, or his seminars, use the following contact information:

The Canfield Companies
P.O. Box 30880 • Santa Barbara, CA 93130
Phone: 805-563-2935 • Fax: 805-563-2945
E-mail: info@jackcanfield.com
Website: www.jackcanfield.com

Who Is Mark Victor Hansen?

In the area of human potential, no one is more respected than Mark Victor Hansen. For more than thirty years, Mark has focused solely on helping people from all walks of life reshape their personal vision of what's possible. His powerful messages of possibility, opportunity, and action have created powerful change in thousands of organizations and millions of individuals worldwide.

He is a sought-after keynote speaker, bestselling author, and marketing maven. Mark's credentials include a lifetime of entrepreneurial success and an extensive academic background. He is a prolific writer with many bestselling books, such as *The One-Minute Millionaire, Cracking the Millionaire Code, How to Make the Rest of Your Life the Best of Your Life, The Power of Focus, The Aladdin Factor,* and *Dare to Win,* in addition to the Chicken Soup for the Soul series. Mark has made a profound influence through his library of audios, videos, and articles in the areas of big thinking, sales achievement, wealth building, publishing success, and personal and professional development.

Mark is the founder of the MEGA Seminar Series. MEGA Book Marketing University and Building Your MEGA Speaking Empire are annual conferences where Mark coaches and teaches new and aspiring authors, speakers, and experts on building lucrative publishing and speaking careers. Other MEGA events include MEGA Info-Marketing and My MEGA Life.

As a philanthropist and humanitarian, Mark works tirelessly for organizations such as Habitat for Humanity, American Red Cross, March of Dimes, Childhelp USA, and many others. He is the recipient of numerous awards that honor his entrepreneurial spirit, philanthropic heart, and business acumen. He is a lifetime member of the Horatio Alger Association of Distinguished Americans, an organization that honored Mark with the prestigious Horatio Alger Award for his extraordinary life achievements.

Mark Victor Hansen is an enthusiastic crusader of what's possible and is driven to make the world a better place.

Mark Victor Hansen & Associates, Inc.
P.O. Box 7665 • Newport Beach, CA 92658
Phone: 949-764-2640 • Fax: 949-722-6912
Website: www.markvictorhansen.com

Who Is Patty Aubery?

As the president of Chicken Soup for the Soul Enterprises and a #1 *New York Times* bestselling coauthor, Patty Aubery knows what it's like to juggle work, family, and social obligations—along with the responsibility of developing and marketing the more than 80 million *Chicken Soup* books and licensed goods worldwide.

She knows because she's been with Jack Canfield's organization since the early days—before Chicken Soup took the country by storm. Jack was still telling these heartwarming stories then, in his training programs, workshops, and keynote presentations, and it was Patty who directed the labor of love that went into compiling and editing the original 101 Chicken Soup stories. Later, she supported the daunting marketing effort and steadfast optimism required to bring it to millions of readers worldwide.

Today, Patty is the mother of two active boys—J. T. and Chandler—exemplifying that special combination of commitment, organization, and life balance all working women want to have. She's been known to finish at the gym by 6:00 AM, guest-host a radio show at 6:30, catch a flight by 9:00 to close a deal—and be back in time for soccer with the kids. But perhaps the most notable accolade for this special working woman is the admiration and love her friends, family, staff, and peers hold for her.

Of her part in the Chicken Soup family, Patty says, "I'm always encouraged, amazed, and humbled by the storytellers I meet when working on any Chicken Soup book, but by far the most poignant have been those stories of women in the working world, overcoming incredible odds and—in the face of all challenges—excelling as only women could do."

Patty is also the coauthor of several other bestselling titles: *Chicken Soup for the Christian Soul, Christian Family Soul,* and *Christian Woman's Soul, Chicken Soup for the Expectant Mother's Soul, Chicken Soup for the Sister's Soul,* and *Chicken Soup for the Surviving Soul.*

She is married to a successful international entrepreneur, Jeff Aubery, and together with J. T. and Chandler they make their home in Santa Barbara, California. Patty can be reached at:

Self-Esteem Seminars
P.O. Box 30880
Santa Barbara, CA 93130
Phone: 805-563-2935
Fax: 805-563-2945

Contributors

We wish to extend our deepest thanks to the following writers and editors whose contributions were vital to the success of this book.

Aaron Bacall has graduate degrees in organic chemistry and educational administration and supervision from New York University. He has been a pharmaceutical research chemist, college department coordinator, college instructor, and cartoonist. His work has appeared in most national publications, and he has contributed to several cartoon collections. His cartoons have been used for advertising, greeting cards, wall calendars, and several corporate promotional books. Three of his cartoons are featured in the permanent collection at Harvard Business School's Baker Library. He continues to create and sell his cartoons. He can be reached at abacall@msn.com.

Nancy Barnes resides with her family in Rowlett, Texas. Formerly a resident of Boardman, Ohio, Nancy has been a registered nurse for thirty-two years. She received great joy in having her first written story published in *Chicken Soup for the Nurse's Soul: A Second Dose*. She hopes to inspire others by sharing her faith and heart through writing.

Inspirational speaker **Lindy Batdorf** shares encouragement nationwide at retreats, business conferences, and workshops on a variety of life-changing topics. She is the author of numerous articles, dramatic presentations, and the humorous parenting book, *Stop and Smell the Asphalt: Laughter and Love Along the Highway of Parenthood*. Contact information available at: www.lindybatdorf.com.

Al Batt is a writer, speaker, storyteller, and humorist living in Minnesota. A newspaper columnist, radio and TV personality, and tour guide, he has received the Ed Franey Conservation Media Award from the Izaak Walton League. Al speaks to anyone who will listen. His mother thinks he is special.

Michelle Borinstein is a professional writer and amateur mother to a large family. Published in newspapers, magazines, anthologies, and online sites, she writes whatever pops into her head: fiction, nonfiction, children's poetry, journalism, features, and occasional shopping lists. Currently looking for an agent for her children's book, she may be reached at mborinstein@013.net.

Ellen Brown is a student at Stonehill College in North Easton, MA where she double majors in English and fine arts. She studied abroad at Oxford University in the fall of 2007 and aspires to pursue a masters degree in creative writing. Ellen also enjoys reconstructing clothing and jewelry.

Debra C. Butler lives in Chesterfield, Virginia, with her husband, Michael, daughter, Ashley, and sons Micheal Lee and Cody Ray. She's worked at the McGuire VA Medical Center in Richmond, Virginia, for over twenty years and currently serves as a program analyst for the office of the chief of staff.

Jennifer Lynn Clay, eighteen, has been published over fifty times in national and international magazines and in several books, including *Chicken Soup for the Preteen Soul 2, Chicken Soup for the Girl's Soul, House Blessings*, and *Forever in Love*. She was a state finalist in the "Power of the Pen" interscholastic writing competition in 2004.

Maril Crabtree is the mother of two and the grandmother of four inspirational children. She lives in Kansas City where she writes nonfiction and poetry, works as an energy practitioner, and teaches yoga. Her website is www.marilcrabtree.com

Lola De Giulio De Maci received her master of arts in education and English from California State University. She loves being a children's author, gathering inspiration from her now-grown children and the many children she has taught over the years. Lola enjoys contributing to Chicken Soup for the Soul books and inspirational speaking. The mother of Maria, Christopher, and Angela, Lola considers motherhood her greatest calling. E-mail: LDeMaci@aol.com.

Mary Emily Dess received her master's degree in English from Sacramento State University and taught English at American River College. She has written for various secular and religious magazines. Mary, her husband, and five children traveled extensively as a military family, including tours of duty to Italy and Korea.

Avis Drucker retired to Cape Cod with husband, Al, as "Washashores" in 2001. Leaving behind corporate life, she quickly discovered writing as her new passion. Her memoir and poetry have been published in *Chicken Soup for the Soul, Prime Time* magazine, *The Philosophical Mother*, the *Cape Cod Times* "On the Road" series, and a Cape anthology entitled *World of Water, World of Sand*. Travel and family visits keep her life full.

Sylvia Duncan spent her first twenty-four years in England and adores her family members on both sides of the Atlantic. She writes for *Sauce* magazine, teaches at Elderhostels in the Ozarks, and conducts writing workshops at a community college. She was previously published in *Chicken Soup for the Father & Daughter Soul*. Contact her at sylvied@juno.com

Teri Elders, LCSW, continues to celebrate active retirement in her country home near Colville, WA. A lifelong freelance writer, she made her Chicken Soup debut with "Easter Bloomers" in *Celebrating Brothers & Sisters*. Her husband, Ken Wilson, two dogs, and three cats provide inspiration, diversion, and distraction. Write her: telders@hotmail.com.

Jackie Fleming is the mother of three and grandmother of many. She has traveled the world on several freighters, and between voyages she e-mails her friends, reads their blogs, and writes at her home in Paradise, California. You can e-mail her at jaxaco@aol.com.

Tessa Floehr lives in Marysville, Ohio, with her husband, Eric, and their daughters, Sophia and Amelia. She teaches part-time at a local preschool. She enjoys writing, cooking, and being a mom. She would like to thank Lori, her writing group partner, for encouraging her to develop this story. Contact: tessa@floehr.com

Betsy Franz is a freelance writer and photographer specializing in the areas of nature, wildlife, the environment, and inspirational human interest topics. You may learn more about Betsy by visiting her website: www.natures details.net

Sally Friedman is a graduate of the University of Pennsylvania. She focuses on family in her writing for national and regional publications. She is the mother of three daughters who often provide inspiration for her essays in the *New York Times, Philadelphia Inquirer,* and *Journal Register* newspapers. Contact: pinegander@aol.com.

Sara Francis-Fujimura is an author from Arizona. Her work has appeared in such magazines as *Girls' Life, Science World, Learning through History, Raising Arizona Kids,* and *Woman's Day,* among others. Sara's young adult historical fiction novel *Whispers from the Desert* won second place in SmartWriters.com's 2007 "Write It Now!" competition. Contact: www.sarafujimura.com.

A graduate of the University of Pennsylvania, **Sally Friedman** focuses on family in her writing for national and regional publications. She is the mother of three daughters who often provide inspiration for her essays in the *New York Times, Philadelphia Inquirer,* and *Journal Register* newspapers. pinegander@aol.com.

Michelle Gannon graduated from Princeton University with a degree in art and archeology. After building up her frequent flier miles as a consultant, she returned to her true passion, the arts. Following graduation with a master's from Columbia, Michelle began teaching Humanities and Film. Currently, Michelle teaches at Temple University in Japan.

Shirley Hailstock's twenty novels have appeared on the *Library Journal, Essence Magazine, 100 Greatest Novels of the 20th Century,* and *Glamour* magazine lists. She holds a Waldenbooks Bestseller Award and a *Romantic Times* magazine Career Achievement Award. Shirley is a past-president of Romance Writers of America. E-mail her at shirley.hailstock@comcast.net

Cynthia Hamond has numerous stories in the Chicken Soup for the Soul series and Multnomah's Stories for the Heart, and other major publications, including *Woman's World* magazine and with King Features Syndication. She received two writing awards and was the featured author in *Anthology Today.* Two stories were made for TV. Contact: www.CynthiaHamond.com.

Patrick Hardin is a freelance cartoonist whose work appears in a variety of books and periodicals in the United States and abroad. He resides in his hometown of Flint, Michigan. He is a graduate of the University of Michigan–Flint, where he earned degrees in philosophy and psychology. He may be contacted at hardin_cartoons@comcast.net.

Ann Weaver Hart is a writer, living in Bryan, Texas. E-mail her at annhart @columnist.com.

Mandy Houk is a freelance writer and editor. She teaches high school literature in Colorado Springs, where she lives with her husband, Pete, and their two daughters. Mandy was born in Georgia and returned to her southern roots when writing her first novel, *Cloud Hunting*. Please visit her website at www.mandyhoulk.com.

Amy Hudock is a single mom who teaches English at a private school in South Carolina. She is the editor in chief of LiteraryMama.com, and coeditor of *Literary Mama: Reading for the Maternally Inclined* (Seal Press, 2006).

Cindy Hval's work has appeared in *Chicken Soup for the Mother and Son Soul, Chicken Soup for the New Mom's Soul,* and *A Cup of Comfort Devotional for Mothers.* She's a correspondent for the *Spokesman Review* newspaper in Spokane, Washington, where she and her husband are raising their four sons. Contact her at dchval@juno.com.

Caroleah Johnson lives in northern California with her husband of thirty-five years. She has two grown children and five grandchildren. A dental hygienist by profession and a writer by passion, she has been published in two other Chicken Soup books and *Upper Room Magazine.* You can reach her at caroleah@gmail.com.

Kim Johnson is a freelance writer and speaker. Her book, *Working Women's Devotions to Go,* was published in 2007, and she has contributed to other compilations. Employed as assistant to a vice president at Disneyland, she and her husband reside in Anaheim, California, and have four children and five grandchildren.

Louise Tucker Jones is an award-winning author and popular speaker. Author/coauthor of three books, her work has been featured in numerous magazines and compilation books, including *Guideposts* and several Chicken Soup titles. Mother of four, grandmother of three, Louise resides in Edmond, Oklahoma. Contact her at LouiseTJ@cox.net or www.LouiseTuckerJones.com.

Jessica Kennedy received her bachelor of arts from the University of California at Davis. At twenty-six, she had a stroke and became a ventilator-dependent quadriplegic. A guest speaker at classes for respiratory therapists and a writer of inspirational articles and children's stories, Jessica foresees a bright future. E-mail her at jessicakennedy1971@yahoo.com.

Nancy Julien Kopp has published stories, articles, personal essays, children's stories, and poetry in magazines, newspapers, e-zines, and in several anthologies, including five Chicken Soup for the Soul books. She is a former teacher who still enjoys teaching through the written word. Nancy lives in the Flint Hills of Kansas with her retired husband.

Susan J. Krom graduated UMASS Dartmouth with a bachelors of science. She is an IT professional and a proud mother. She has always enjoyed writing poetry and was inspired by the pregnancy of her first child to write the poem in this book.

Margaret Lang is the author of twenty-eight published stories, many with Chicken Soup. She is a full-time teacher/missionary to youth and adults in the United States, Africa, and Asia. Her teachings can be heard on legacyradioonline.com. She is a mother of two and a grandmother of three.

Lyn Larsen lives in rural Alberta in Canada. She studied social work in the early seventies and received her B.Ed in English in the nineties. She has worked as a social worker and a teacher. She writes mainly for teens and served as editor for her writers' club's latest publication.

Heather McAlvey lives in Walnut, Illinois, with her son, Brendan. She, along with her family, are avid baseball fans who are still waiting for "next year" to arrive! She also enjoys photography, scrapbooking, and writing. She is a restaurant manager.

Sandra McGarrity lives and writes in Chesapeake, Virginia. She is the author of three novels. Her writing has appeared in many publications, and she maintains a weekly column at TidewaterCrossSection.com, where she is a member of the Tidewater Christian Writers Forum. Visit her web page at hometown.aol.com/mygr8m8/myhomepage/books.html

Paula McKee lives in Ontario, Canada, with her husband and two kids. Among other freelance writing projects, Paula writes a first-person parenting column for her area's local newspaper. Life with kids, she finds, produces a constant flow of entertaining anecdotes that parents can relate to. Reach her at paula.homefront@gmail.com.

Lynn Meade, Instructor of Communication, is inspired daily by her sons, Taylor and Titus, who encourage her to find joy in the small things. Her parents continue to fuel her passion to write and her husband, John, supplies the daily hugs needed to keep her going. familymeade@hotmail.com.

Emily Mendell is a graduate of the University of Pennsylvania. She fills her days working in public affairs and playing as much as possible with her husband and two young sons. Her essays and articles have been published in the *Philadelphia Inquirer* and on iparenting.com. Please e-mail her at emilymendell@aol.com.

Jennifer Oliver, from Copperas Cove, Texas, dedicates this story to her magnificent, creative life forces: Cody, Ethan, Matthew, and Madison. Jennifer's stories have appeared in several Chicken Soup books and other heartwarming publications.

Celeste T. Palermo lives in Colorado with her husband, Pete, and daughters, Peyton and Morgan. She is the author of *From the Red Tees* (Cumberland House, 2007). She writes for various magazines and is a newspaper columnist and contributing author to *Chicken Soup for the Woman Golfer's Soul*. Visit her at www.celestepalermo.com.

Valerie J. Palmer is best known in the Peace River area of Alberta, Canada, for her artwork and mushroom spore prints. She has enjoyed writing poetry ever since she was a child in war-time England. This poem was written after her own mother's death from Alzheimer's and is dedicated to all caregivers.

Mark Parisi's "off the mark" comic, syndicated since 1987, is distributed by United Media. Mark's humor also graces greeting cards, T-shirts, calendars, magazines, newsletters, and books. Check out: www.offthemark.com Lynn is his wife/business partner. Their daughter, Jen, contributes with inspiration (as do three cats).

Saralee Perel is an award-winning writer, chosen as such in the National Society of Newspaper Columnists' competition. She's a *Family Circle* magazine contributor and a nationally syndicated columnist. Her novel, *Raw Nerves*, received the BookSense honor. Saralee's favorite activity is giving and receiving back rubs with her loving husband, Bob. E-mail: sperel@saraleeperel.com.

Stephanie Piro lives in New Hampshire with her husband, daughter, and three cats. She is one of King Features' team of women cartoonists, "Six Chix" (she is the Saturday chick!). Her single panel, "Fair Game," appears in newspapers and on her website www.stephaniepiro.com. Her book *My Cat Loves Me Naked* is available at bookstores everywhere. She also designs gift items for her company Strip T's. Contact her at stephaniepiro@verizon.net.

Joyce Rapier, author of several books and short stories, resides in Arkansas. Joyce, president and owner of Rapier Inc., a business forms/ad specialty company, enjoys writing, gardening, oil painting, and her family. Joyce has three children and seven grandchildren (one deceased). You may contact Joyce through www.authorsden.com/jpycelrapier.

Carol McAdoo Rehme never played nurse or bandaged her dolls. She advised her kids to save their accidents for their dad's attention. Now a grandma, she's relieved to pass the torch of responsibility to the next generation. Carol is a prolific writer, editor, and coauthor of numerous gift books. Her latest project, *Chicken Soup for the Empty Nester's Soul*, will be released in 2008. Contact her at carol@rehme.com.

Natalie June Reilly is a newspaper columnist and the author of the children's book, *My Stick Family: Helping Children Cope with Divorce*. She is a single mother of two handsome teenage boys, the loves of her life! She loves most to travel with them, seeing the world through their eyes.

Gwen Rockwood is a freelance writer living in Arkansas with her husband and three kids. Her weekly column appears in several newspapers in Arkansas and Missouri and has been published for more than ten years. Contact her at rockwoodfiles@cox.net.

Sallie A. Rodman is an award-winning writer whose work has appeared in many Chicken Soup anthologies. She has three grown children and resides with her husband in Los Alamitos, California. Sallie says she gets her love of family traditions from her mom and hopes her children continue them long into the future. E-mail her at sa.rodman@verizon.net.

Tammy Ruggles is a freelance writer based in Kentucky. She writes short stories, articles, and screenplays. Her first book, *Peace*, was published in 2005.

Harriet May Savitz is the award-winning author of twenty-six books, including *Run, Don't Walk*, an ABC Afterschool Special produced by Henry Winkler. Several of her books about the disabled (YA, fiction, nonfiction) have been reissued by AuthorsGuild/iUniverse and can be found at www.iUniverse.com or www.harrietmaysavitz.com. Contact her at hmaysavitz@aol.com or at Essay Books at www.authorhouse.com.

Joanne Wright Schulte has been writing for five years and has been published in *Chicken Soup for the Soul Celebrating Mothers and Daughters*. She loves music, reading, and writing, and is active in her garden club and various church activities. She holds a bachelor's degree in sociology.

Lori Shaw-Cohen is a bestselling author, editor, and nationally published journalist whose work has spanned almost three decades. Formerly the managing editor of *Teen* Magazine, her books include the national bestseller *Home Buying by the Experts* and *The Princess and the PMS*. Contact Lori at ALoudVoice@aol.com.

Sarah Smiley is a syndicated newspaper columnist and author of *Going Overboard* (New American Library, 2005). She is the mother of three young boys. Website: www.SarahSmiley.com.

Pamela Gayle Smith lives in Mount Vernon, Indiana, and has been married to John since 1969. They have three daughters—Shannon, Jennifer, and Misti.They are grandparents to eight grandchildren—Nicholas, Tara, Austin, Seth, Averie, Johnathan, Brandon, and Zachery. She enjoys reading, traveling, and meeting new people. She can be e-mailed at IndianaRhymer@aol.com.

Diane Stark is a teacher, a writer, a wife, and a mother. She lives in southern

Indiana with her husband, Eric, and their four children. She loves writing about parenting and family issues, and her favorite topic is, of course, her own kids. Please email her at DianeStark19@yahoo.com.

Elva Stoelers is an award-winning Canadian writer and a proud contributor to a number of Chicken Soup titles. As well as being broadcast on CBC radio, her work has been published internationally in a variety of parenting magazines. She has tried to emulate her mother's enthusiasm for child rearing while raising her own three children and is happy to report that eccentricity appears to be genetic.

Rachel Lee Stuart got her degree in psychology from Appalachian State University. She lives in Durham, North Carolina, with her husband and son. Rachel enjoys music, cake decorating, and working with the elderly. Her faith and her family are the most important things in her life.

Beverly A. Suntjens is a wife, mother, recreation therapist, instructor, writer, and speaker. She received her bachelor of arts from the University of Alberta and has completed her first children's novel, but her greatest accomplishment is that her two sons and one daughter call her "Mom." E-mail her at sunnyandbev@yahoo.com.

Ken Swarner is the author of *Whose Kids Are These Anyway?* He can be reached at kenswarner@aol.com.

Marcia M. Swearingen is a former newspaper editor and columnist, now freelancing full-time. Her stories have appeared in *Guideposts* magazine, other Chicken Soup and Cup of Comfort books, and numerous local publications. She and her husband, Jim, have been married thirty-six years. They have one daughter and a new son-in-law! E-mail: mswearingen@comcast.net.

AnnMarie Tait lives in Conshohocken, Pennsylvania, with her husband, Joe, and Sammy the "Wonder Yorkie." In addition to writing stories about her large Irish Catholic family, Annmarie enjoys singing and recording Irish and American Folk Songs. "Autumn Leaves" is the third story published in the Chicken Soup for the Soul series. Email her at irishbloom@aol.com.

Cristy Trandahl works as a freelance writer while raising six beautiful children. Cristy's stories have been published in dozens of nationally distributed anthologies including Chicken Soup, Cup of Comfort, and Breastfeeding Diaries. Visit her website at www.cristytrandahl.com.

Kathryn Veliky received her bachelor of arts in drama from Pace University. She currently works for the meetings and events division of Carlson Marketing and is an independent consultant for the Traveling Vineyard. She lives with her husband, Michael, daughter, Dorian, and two dogs in New Jersey. Kathryn enjoys camping, canoeing, traveling, cooking, board games, and wine tasting.

Beth K. Vogt is the author of *Baby Changes Everything: Embracing and Preparing for Motherhood after 35.* She's learned to enjoy life all over the parenting spectrum with children ages twenty-four, twenty-one, nineteen, and seven. Contact Beth at beth@mommycomelately.com.

Bob Vojtko makes a living poking fun at the human condition through his cartoons. You'll find his cartoons in newspapers, newsletters, magazines, books, and on the Internet. Bob lives in Strongville, Ohio, with his wife, Susan, and their Boston terrier, Massie.

Beverly F. Walker enjoys writing, photography, scrapbooking, and being with her grandchildren. Her stories appear in *Angel Cats: Divine Messengers of Comfort, Chicken Soup for the Cat Lover's Soul,* and *Chicken Soup for the Soul in Menopause.*

Stefanie Wass lives in Hudson, Ohio, with her husband and two daughters. Her writing has appeared in *Chicken Soup for the New Mom's Soul, Chicken Soup for the Beach Lover's Soul,* the *Christian Science Monitor,* the *Akron Beacon Journal,* and other newspapers nationwide. Contact Stefanie via e-mail at swass@adelphia.net.

Verna Wood has published articles about her battle with breast cancer and the prison ministry about which she is passionate. She is an investigative reporter for the *US Observer Oklahoma.* She can be contacted at Reno ssnowflake@sbcglobal.net.

Chicken Soup African American Soul
Chicken Soup African American Woman's Soul
Chicken Soup Breast Cancer Survivor's Soul
Chicken Soup Bride's Soul
Chicken Soup Caregiver's Soul
Chicken Soup Cat Lover's Soul
Chicken Soup Christian Family Soul
Chicken Soup College Soul
Chicken Soup Couple's Soul
Chicken Soup Dieter's Soul
Chicken Soup Dog Lover's Soul
Chicken Soup Entrepreneur's Soul
Chicken Soup Expectant Mother's Soul
Chicken Soup Father's Soul
Chicken Soup Fisherman's Soul
Chicken Soup Girlfriend's Soul
Chicken Soup Golden Soul
Chicken Soup Golfer's Soul, Vol. I, II
Chicken Soup Horse Lover's Soul, Vol. I, II
Chicken Soup Inspire a Woman's Soul
Chicken Soup Kid's Soul, Vol. I, II
Chicken Soup Mother's Soul, Vol. I, II
Chicken Soup Parent's Soul
Chicken Soup Pet Lover's Soul
Chicken Soup Preteen Soul, Vol. I, II
Chicken Soup Scrapbooker's Soul
Chicken Soup Sister's Soul, Vol. I, II
Chicken Soup Shopper's Soul
Chicken Soup Soul, Vol. I-VI
Chicken Soup at Work
Chicken Soup Sports Fan's Soul
Chicken Soup Teenage Soul, Vol. I-IV
Chicken Soup Woman's Soul, Vol. I, II

To order direct: Telephone (800) 441-5569 • www.hcibooks.com
Prices do not include shipping and handling. Your response code is CCS.